The Servant Church

Diaconal Ministry
and the Episcopal Church

John E. Booty

Morehouse-Barlow Co., Wilton, Connecticut

Morehouse-Barlow Co., Inc.
78 Danbury Road
Wilton, Connecticut 06897

ISBN 0-8192-1316-0

Library of Congress Catalog Card Number 82-81429

Printed in the United States of America

Contents

Foreword

This book by John Booty comes at a most helpful moment for those struggling with building and living a deeper theological understanding of ministry. For the past decade, the Church has been attempting to integrate a growing appreciation of mutual ministry with major advances in biblical scholarship and liturgical changes. Central to this effort has been the development and support of the ministry of the laity. The dramatic changes in the Church's understanding and perception of the ministry of the laity have raised many questions about the meaning of priesthood, ordained diaconate ministry and the episcopacy. Today we have both experience of a wide variety of new models of ministry and a growing body of theological literature and related scholarship. Many of us believe this is the time of synthesis and reintegration of all that has been so challenged. Our problem is to discover how to weave everything together: biblical scholarship, history, ecclesiology and living it out as ministry faithful to the calling of Jesus Christ in this time and place. I believe this manuscript is a most useful tool for diocesan and parish leaders, Commissions on Ministry and others to make sense of where they are and what is needed for their next steps in ministry development.

The usefulness of this book will not be as a "how-to-do-it" manual on ministry development. More importantly it offers a set of theological and historical criteria by which we can examine our own assumptions and experiences regarding ministry. You can push against this book, argue with it, learn from it and benefit from the exchange. It offers a foundation for building a coherent set of answers to the questions of the times:

- what is mutual accountability between clergy and laity?
- what is servant ministry?
- what are the inadequacies in our present ministry support systems if we are serious about servant ministry?
- what is the role of a Diocesan Commission on Ministry?
- how do we distinguish between the ministry *of* the church, *to* the church, and *by* the church?
- what are the changing roles and responsibilities of bishops?

- why do we need more people ordained to the permanent diaconate if we have a well developed ministry of the laity?

It is this last question that is being given very serious attention by the Church over the next four years. Nine dioceses are participating in a study of the diaconal ministry being conducted by the Council for the Development of Ministry (CDM). This study will examine all phases of recruitment, selection, training, deployment and accountability of deacons. Particular attention will be given to relationships between deacons and the laity, priests and bishops. The study will attempt to determine in what ways ordained diaconal ministry supports or detracts from the servant ministry of the whole church.

The CDM recognized the need for this book as a resource for anyone interested in servant ministry participating in the study. CDM leaders asked John Booty if he would write such a book based on his research and lecturing on the subject over the past several years. Fortunately, he agreed. What followed was a collaboration of sorts. As sections of the manuscript were written they were shared with readers within the CDM membership who are much involved with developing diaconal ministry. Out of this dialogue came successive drafts and now the completed book. The book is being distributed widely by the CDM to all those helping in the study, and recommended to the whole church for use as a ministry development resource.

The CDM membership is grateful to John Booty for his response to this request. It serves the purposes of our study on diaconal ministry in the best possible way. We are also aware that this is a book for the whole church to use for its ongoing and exciting reassessment of ministry.

Barry Menuez
Council for the Development of Ministry
The Episcopal Church

Chapter 1.

The Church
in the Present

The World Situation

The world situation in which the church exists, of which it is a part, to which it is sent with the Word of judgment and salvation, is one of great danger and great potential.

It is probably true that the same could be said of any critical time in the past. The ancient world of the church's infancy, for instance, was witnessing the old age and dissolution of the Roman Empire. It was a time of wars, intrigues, persecution of minorities such as Christians, and a growing inability to hold together the massive political, social and spiritual apparatus constituting the empire. At the same time, however, there was great potential. Principally, there were laws, culture, and the Christian faith which in time conquered the empire's barbarian conquerors and paved the way for a new unity, a civilization which we call medieval and associate with the magnificent, fragile harmony and order of Cathedrals and theological summas, with the glittering courts of Charlemagne and Eleanor of Aquitaine, with a marvelous variety of Christians, such as Catherine of Sienna, Francis of Assisi, Thomas Aquinas and Julian of Norwich.

Viewing the ancient world with its dangers and potentialities some modern observers are struck by ways in which the present world situation resembles the waning days of the Roman Empire. And yet, while acknowledging the similarities, it is difficult to repress the feeling that now the dangers are greater. We may also affirm that the potential is greater too, but then many would add that it is also more dubious. The feeling may exist because it is always more difficult to understand the course and meaning of events still developing and it is more difficult, if not altogether impossible to peer into the future and to predict with accuracy where we are heading. Not that we are without any recourse in this regard. We have the expertise of modern technology, computer science, and system analysis and dynamics; we have psycho-social experts, highly skilled in analyzing human behavior and predicting its future course; and we have our prophets, religious and political. But we can never be certain of the accuracy of such experts until the present is past and the future is present.

What we do know is that people of all sorts, dispersed around the globe, share common impressions of the present danger confronting us all. Most important is the threat of annihilation hanging over us like a great, burgeoning, mushroom cloud casting a shadow over all of life. Nuclear proliferation and the accumulation of nuclear weaponry continue ominously while control and disarmament discussions falter and stagnate. There is no solace in being told that in the event of a nuclear attack some of us would survive.

The threat of annihilation feeds those anxieties that eat away the heart of the civilization and the hearts of individuals. Such anxiety permeates the conferences of world leaders and the gatherings of citizens in cities and villages around the world. It is an anxiety often masked, buried, stridently denied, but it is there consuming us. In such an atmosphere the warfare and terrorism, riots and assassinations that plague peoples around the earth are intensified.

The world situation is one in which the interdependence of nations, enemies as well as friends is growing. Increasingly nations are forced to acknowledge their dependence upon resources controlled by others. Sometimes they cooperate, but often they compete and their competition turns into conflict, economic and military. In the process nationalism is reasserted, weakening the efforts made through the United Nations and elsewhere to promote international cooperation and peace.

The world situation is also one in which, to our astonishment you can have both inflation and depression, a rising standard of living and a worsening of poverty. Within blocks of one another in some of the world's great cities we can find incredible wealth and equally incredible poverty. The ghettos of the rich and of the poor are secured by vigilant police and others. Neither are secure against the anxiety of our age and the fear of annihilation.

The world situation is such, according to some prophets, dubbed prophets of doom, that if we are not destroyed by war we shall be destroyed by greed and by the inevitable consequences of exponential growth, that is growth such as that of the world's population which occurs geometrically, escalating in such a fashion as to boggle the mind. Such prophets speak of a coming world of scarcity, a world already in our midst to some degree, in which survival will depend in large degree upon our reaching some sort of equilibrium, building the steady state society of zero sum growth. When we ponder the possibility that such prophets may be right and wonder how we can do anything about a situation so massive and complex our anxiety grows further.

We are aware of the dangers in the world situation and to a degree find verification of what we observe on a global scale in our personal experience. We are plagued by doubts concerning self-identity and fear that if we probe too deeply we shall find in our selves nothing of substance. At best, we conclude in our darkest moments, in our depths we are bland, at worst we are void. Self-doubt extends to interpersonal relationships, to family life, if we have any family, and to those intimate networks that form and dissolve with terrifying rapidity, confirming our suspicion that there is, after all, very little reason to hope. If we are lucky we succeed in avoiding such awareness, working, playing, fantasizing with great intensity, living for the momentary pleasure, seeking that which is immediately satisfying, largely indifferent to the consequences.

In the macrocosm of global and national life, in the microcosm of personal and interpersonal existence we are beset by the threat of annihilation—the dissolution of world and national order and of the consciousness-centered personality.

But we also dream dreams of a utopian future. We acknowledge that this is an age of amazing potential. If we can stave off catastrophe there is no limit to what humanity can achieve before the end of the century. We are a people whose faith in progress has been repeatedly shaken by war, by economic depression, and much else, but the realities of the recent past provide a basis for hope that we shall progress further in our time toward the building of a society in which happiness shall prevail.

The growth of communications and transportation has helped to create a greater interdependence among the nations of the earth, thus bringing us ever nearer to the realization of a world order in which justice and peace shall prevail. The threat of nuclear annihilation—ever escalating with the increase of nuclear proliferation and the arms race—provides a forceful deterrent to war and increases the pressures upon the world powers to reach accord on control and disarmament. Nuclear power itself possesses great potential for meeting our energy needs; we have only to solve its attendant problems, such as security and the disposal of poisonous wastes.

Science and technology have opened new vistas for mankind. The space program has opened a new frontier and produced spin-offs that have enhanced life on earth. Dependence upon fossil fuels, a finite resource for energy and goods, is gradually being replaced by solar power, geothermal, wind and recycled energy—energy that is virtually infinite and at least sufficient to provide the needs for an expanding world population far, far into the future, at least for as long a time as human history has run to this date.

We have made immense strides in our perpetual struggle against the ravages of disease. Genetic research, carefully controlled, can help us to improve the human condition. We are achieving significant success in the controlling population growth, largely through the various means of birth control. We are making progress in increasing the agricultural production of the world needed to overcome poverty and to provide sustenance. New, more wholesome crops, cybernated food production, and the like are being developed.

Furthermore, progress has been made in education. Illiteracy around the world is declining. We have achieved much toward the eradication of racial and sexual discrimination. As individuals we possess a greater freedom under the law than did our ancestors, freedom to be what we are and what we would be without fear and without dissimulation. We have far to go, but we are realizing our potential. We have reason to hope for the future.

This hope extends deep into our selves. We recognize the blandness, the void, and thus there is a yearning, a seeking, a strong desire for something to give us a sense of being, of worth, of meaning and purpose. And so we seek through self-help programs, group therapies, transcendental meditation, and a vast catalog of spiritual ventures, for that which we believe with all of the force of our will to live to exist. Life is worth living. What we need is some understanding of who we are, such an understanding as shall give us hope for the future, such hope as shall influence the present for good.

The Church

The church tends to reflect the condition of the society in which it exists. This should not be surprising. It is, after all, an institution and as such is a part of the culture as well as being a people set apart constituting the people of God. All of the fears and hopes we have discussed may be found in the church for the church is people, a portion of the earth's population with all of earth's dangers and potentiality.

We are at one and the same time members of the church and of a particular race, sex, nationality—whatever serves to constitute our identity as humans. Being Christians does not mean that we cease to be human. Hopefully it means that we are more fully human, that is to say, more fully that which God created as human.

It is quite natural, then, that as the church we should reflect the fears and anxieties associated with the threat of annihilation, global and personal. It is natural, too, that we should reflect the hope associated with the positive gains humanity has achieved and is yet to achieve through science and technology in personal and interpersonal, national and international affairs. As the church we are worried about nuclear proliferation and personal disintegration. We are concerned to promote peace with justice, to liberate the oppressed, to feed the hungry, to relieve the sick, and live responsibly in our ecosystem.

Furthermore, there are dangers and potentialities associated with the present condition of our institutional life. As Christians we recognize our interdependence, local and global, but in spite of the ecumenical movement over the past century we are still divided into churches, denominations and sects. We still compete with one another for members, money and prestige. We are preoccupied with growth, for success in our culture is measured in terms of growth. Therefore the signs of weakness in the institution cause worry and pain. Decreasing numbers relative to the expanding population with the correlative shrinkage of monetary and other resources provoke us to defeatist attitudes so that in our weakness we grow weaker. Churches which once had curates now have none. Churches which once had rectors now make do with part-time or non-stipendiary clergy. We rationalize our present condition, but it worries us greatly, nevertheless, and contributes to our fear that we are without influence in our society, in our world.

Our anxiety causes us to turn inward, to be more concerned for how to make ourselves attractive than for mission—Christ's mission. We circulate questionnaires designed to discover what is wanted of the church in a particular place with the implied intent of providing whatever is wanted: shorter sermons and services, more parish calling, more youth work, and the like. If we provide what is wanted it is suggested that we will gain more members, have more money, and be on the whole vastly more successful. Thus we more and more forcefully reflect the society in which we exist, turning the Gospel of Jesus Christ into culture-Christianity, providing some escape from the dangers of this age while harboring this age's anxiety.

But the church is not exclusively identified with the present world situation. It is God's people, the extension of the incarnate Christ in history, the vehicle of the Holy Spirit. The church transcends its environment while participating in it, transcends to judge and to heal. The potential is in our midst, as we are set apart through Baptism and empowered through Word and Sacrament to be God's agents working in the midst of our world's dangers and potentialities, that we and all we may influence may become more nearly that which is intended to be.

We know that the potential is there, because it is manifested in ways too numerous to catalog. We witness in the same questionnaires and in parochial self studies the quest of the church's people for meaning, for healing, and for hope. A literate, sophisticated Episcopalian in Cleveland pled for help from the church in dealing with world issues. He acknowledged that in the Middle East and in Northern Ireland religion was playing a part in the strife. Who would help him understand? A parishioner in Louisiana pled for spiritual guidance, asking how she could learn to pray when her doubt was so strong and her perplexity over life was so acute. A student in one of our seminaries, preparing for ordination and about to graduate, asked who am I, what am I doing, where do I turn for help? People in the church, people who constitute the church, are asking the vital questions and where such questions are being raised there is life, there is potential for hope and direction.

We witness, too, the potential in the church's active participation and at times crucial leadership in the struggles for civil rights, women's liberation, international justice and peace. We witness the potential in the church's struggles against nuclear proliferation and the arms race, against anti-semitism and all infractions of human rights, against poverty and hunger and all that denies to humans access to the basic stuff of life. The potential is there, too, in the church's commitment to the spirit of ecumenicity, a commitment that wavers but never dies. It is there in the church's refusal to abandon the urban ghettos and to turn away from the plight of our cities.

The potential is there as expressed in various movements for renewal and revitalization, in the struggle for concrete recognition of the ministry of the laity and for mutual ministry, in the stubborn and spirited movement to recover the ancient diaconate of the church, in the revision and renewal of the church's liturgy, in events and groups committed to the recovery of the church's spirituality.

The church is alive and lively. Beyond its manifold anxieties there is growing a spirit of rebirth and renewal which is the chief sign in our time of hope not only for the church itself but for the society in which the church exists. We know this to be true for we have witnessed the vitality of the Spirit working in the lives of countless numbers of people who serve God in Jesus Christ, whose lives and deaths have mirrored the life and death of Jesus Christ and have ministered thus to our need. For our time and our communion let the witness of Janani Luwum be our symbol. This human being, the Archbishop of Uganda, Rwanda, Burundi and Boga-Zaire in East Africa, defied the forces of evil and in his passion and death at the hands of Idi Amin witnessed to Jesus Christ, going the way that Jesus went, raising up in the midst of darkness a light, illuminating the present to reveal its meaning and the future revealing its hope.

That same meaning and hope is present in the holy routine of the church, a routine that holds constantly before us the meaning and hope made known to us and to the world in Jesus Christ.

The holy routine involves the church's worship and witness, the *Book of Common Prayer*, the extension of that worship in care for the needy, in the healing of broken spirits, minds and bodies, in education that prepares people to deal creatively with the world's dangers and potentialities, and in prophetic witness against evil and in behalf of the right insofar as we are enabled and able to discern the right. And there is prayer, ceaselessly rising, directing our minds and hearts, inspiring our actions, opening us to the Spirit that sets us on fire with zeal to be and to do in obedience to God's will.

There are those who say that much of our worship and work in the name of God is essentially egotistic and self-serving. There are those who point out that our involvement in causes such as civil rights and women's liberation is reactive, not from the heart, but provoked by the strident demands of the enslaved and oppressed. They further indicate that too often, once the agitation ceases, we sink back into our former complacence, acquiescing once more to injustice. There are those who believe that the church really is irrelevant or worse, that it has contributed to the worsening human situation. It has been learnedly reported that the modern exploitation of nature is rooted in the doctrine that God created nature for our use, a doctrine that need not lead to exploitation but that given the human condition inevitably does. Such doctrine has had disastrous results both for our environment and for the human spirit. It has also been learnedly reported that Christianity is largely responsible for anti-semitism, for racism and for sexism.

Whatever truth there is in such accusations witnesses to the fallibility, the finitude, the sin of the church. The church can be and has often been apostate. It has been in the power of evil. In order to pray aright the church must first confess its sin and ask for forgiveness, for conversion and renewal.

It seems clear that for the church to be the church—God's own people—it must not only confess its sin. It must also be on guard, constantly concerned to distinguish between that which is of God and that which is not, always aware of the dubiety involved in so distinguishing. On the basis of this necessity the church's educational programs are built and pursued, for if the church is to be the church it must be steeped in that which is of God and committed to the same in spite of the inevitable pain involved.

There is another sin. That is the acceptance of the criticism in such a way that we crumble and fade. The church as an earthly institution peopled by fallible humans contributes to the world's crises, but the church as the people of God does not, but rather is dedicated to the alleviating of the world's ills. "God sent the Son into the world, not to condemn the world, but that the world through him might be saved" (John 3:17).

The Church's Role in the World Situation

One of the significant facts of this age is that in the midst of the world's complexity, with its dangers and potential, voices are heard calling out for that which the church alone can adequately provide. Dr. Philip Potter of the World Council of Churches, at a Conference on Faith, Science and the Future, held in this country in 1979, remarked that it is the scientists and technologists "who are posing acute ethical questions to the churches and theologians." He added that our "traditional categories are hardly adequate to the enterprise," but that does nothing to decrease the challenge.[1]

In 1968 the Club of Rome began an international effort at planning for the future of planet earth. Its first report, *Limits To Growth* (1972), aroused a furor by predicting disaster if our commitment to growth continued while population was dramatically expanding and the world's resources needed to sustain life rapidly dwindled. In 1974 a second report, *Mankind at the Turning Point*, was published with urgent recommendations for a dramatic revolution in human values. The report urged the development of world consciousness whereby individuals identify themselves with global society rather than national units, a new ethic whereby humans achieve greater satisfaction from saving or conserving resources rather than from spending and wasting, a new attitude toward nature whereby we seek not conquest but cooperation viewing ourselves as a part of nature, and concern for future generations such concern as causes us to surrender present possessions that future generations may have sufficient to sustain life.[2] Perceptive observers acknowledged that such values are to be found in Holy Scripture and have been taught more or less successfully in the church for centuries. The report clearly challenged the church to promote more vigorously and in commanding ways that which lay close to its heart.

In *Goals for Mankind* (1977), another report to the Club of Rome, Christianity was specifically mentioned, along with other world religions. First, the great influence of Christianity among the leaders of the world was acknowledged, this in spite of the ways some outside and within the church disclaim any effective influence for good. Those drafting the report were convinced that the church's message and teaching is of utmost importance for the world. Two things were noted as positive values, the universal character of Christianity (it is and always has been essentially global), and its strong ethical emphasis. Christianity has staying power "as a universal religion, relevant to all men without distinction of nation, race or caste."[3] Christianity possesses a strong ethic, such an ethic as is needed for the future: "To be at one with God is to have the mind of Christ, who went about doing good. The marks of the Kingdom of God are justice and mercy, forgiveness, sharing, self-sacrifice on behalf of all who are in physical or spiritual need, and brotherhood with no distinctions of class or race. 'By this shall all men know that ye are my disciples, if ye have love to one another.' "[4] The report does not dwell on the failure of Christians to live up to such an ethic. It rather dwells on the positive applications of the ethic by Christians and Christian organizations such as the World Council of Churches to the global issues that confront us all.

One of the important participants in shaping the early reports to the Club of Rome was Jay W. Forrester, an Episcopalian, professor of management at the Massachusetts Institute of Technology, developer of a methodology called "system dynamics"—a means of determining the bases on which we act as humans in society—and of a computerized world model that has been the basis for much analysis and projection. Forrester believes that as in a corporation a strong manager is responsible for maintaining long-range values on the basis of which short-range decisions can most adequately be made, so for society at large and for the emerging global community the responsibility for maintaining long-range values rests with religion, and most specifically with the church. "The institution with the longest time horizon is in the best technical position to lead in exploring the nature of the social system; the church should establish that distant horizon. Long-term values are closely tied to what society is to be one hundred, or two hundred, or one thousand years hence. If not the church, who is to look that far ahead? But," he goes on to say, "the church is in the predicament of undergoing a shortening time horizon when it should be turning attention to a horizon beyond that of any other unit in the society."[5]

We need not look solely to the Club of Rome, its experts and its reports for evidence that the church is being called upon to provide long range values and a vision of the future. We can, indeed, look to those who oppose the limits to growth line of reasoning with its prediction of a coming age of scarcity. F. M. Esfandiary of the New School of Social Research in New York has argued that what is needed is not the limitation of growth but dedication to growth for there is in humanity the potential for endless growth. We have the resources and expertise to produce unlimited affluence and happiness, he said. But Esfandiary at the same time recognized the fundamental human quandry in terms of values when he wrote: "Let it be well understood that people around the world fester in scarcity not because we lack resources. But because we still squander billions of dollars on armaments."[6] He does not pursue the point in the article quoted but it seems apparent that if spending on armaments is to decrease, let alone cease, there has to be a changed ethic, a vision of the future dominated by values that influence and guide present decisions. And there is no institution in the world today with more ability to do what is needed now than the Christian church. We surely cannot look to science and technology for the fulfillment of our deepest needs. With reference to the possibility of all out nuclear war, the scientists Wiesner and York wrote that: "Both sides in the arms race are . . . confronted by the dilemma of steadily increasing military power and steadily decreasing national security. *It is our considered professional judgment that this dilemma has no technical solution.* If the great powers continue to look for solutions in the area of science and technology only, the result will be to worsen the situation."[7]

How are we to identify the heart and core of what the church has to offer? The answer is suggested by the way in which scientists and technologists refer to the need for cooperation and self-sacrifice, involving the surrender of arrogant nationalism in the name of world consciousness, world peace and justice, the surrender of present pleasures for the sake of future generations, and the surrender of human pride for the sake of caring for that nature on which we depend, of which we are a part, and for which we are responsible before God. The heart and core of what the church must offer is identified with the very personality of its Lord and of the people who constitute the body of forgiven sinners empowered with Good News for the world. The heart and core is *diakonia* for which the long neglected Order of Deacons stands as an empowering symbol and instrument. We turn now to reflect upon the Biblical and theological understanding of the Church as Servant.

Chapter 2.

The Biblical Vision
of the Church as Servant

The Heart of Jesus' Teaching

The church has been variously described. It is the Body of Christ, the extension of the Incarnation in history, the Bride of Christ, and so on and on. With the recent development of biblical theology the concept of the people of God has gained popularity, for as a concept it is rooted in the Old Testament, referring to Israel, and finds expression in the New Testament with reference to the "New Israel." Vatican II adopted another metaphor calling the church a sacrament, meaning that it is a sign and instrument, signifying the creative unity of all God's people with God in Christ.

Here, however, another metaphor is adopted, one that seems more adequate and responsive to the dangers and potentialities of the present world situation. The Church is Servant. That is to say, it is that community in the world that serves God and God's creation, and in particular humanity.

In this sense the church is the body of Christ, for its life of service is the extension of Christ's ministry as servant in time and space—in all of history and throughout all the world. The fundamental reason for the being of the church is service. As Karl Barth said: "Service is not just one of the determinations of the being of the community. It is its being in all its functions. Nothing that is done or takes place can escape the question whether and how far within it the community serves its Lord and His work in the world, and its members serve one another by mutual liberation for participation in the service of the whole."[1] Without service the church ceases to be that which it was created to be. This is the message of the New Testament.

The church is most adequately defined in relation to its founder, Jesus Christ, who he is and what he does. It is clear, according to the records, that in his own mind and in the minds of those most perceptive around him and following after him he is the servant of God and of God's people.

Following the Lukan account of the Last Supper, the disciples began to argue concerning "which of them was to be regarded as the greatest." Jesus, dismayed and perhaps angered, pained by the misunderstanding of his little band, commented:

> The kings of the Gentiles exercise lordship over them; and those in authority over them are called benefactors. But not so with you; rather let the greatest among you become as the youngest, and the leader as one who serves. For which is the greater, one who sits at table, or one who serves? Is it not one who sits at table? But I am among you as one who serves (Luke 22:25-27).

The Greek word for "service" in this passage is *diakoneō*, the word from which, in its noun form, *diakonos*, the words diaconate and deacon come. In its earliest recorded use the word concerned waiting on table or, more generally, caring for or providing for the needs of others.

Among the ancient Greeks such service was not looked upon with favor. Only service rendered to the state was respected. Callicles, in Plato's *Gorgias*, expressed the Greek sentiment concerning ordinary service when he asked: "How can a man be happy who is the servant of anything?"[2] To rule—not serve —is the basis of the greatest human happiness. Compared to those who practice the arts of medicine and gymnastics, servants such as bakers, cooks, weavers, shoemakers, and the like, are "servile and menial and illiberal."

The Jews at first took an opposite view of service. The relation between the master and the servant was highly esteemed, the more so when the master was great, especially when the master was God. The Hebrew *ebed*, which can be translated as servant or slave, was used positively of the "servants of the Lord." Israel was "my servant" because it was the chosen people of God. The "servant poems" of Isaiah 42:1-4, 49:1-6, 50:4-9, and 52:13-53:12, are associated with the servant who fulfills his divine mission, suffering and dying for the sins of others.

In later Judaism, service was less highly regarded. It is this decline of regard for service that Jesus attacked in the parable of the Good Samaritan and elsewhere. The commandment to love, and thus to serve one's neighbors was absolute in the religion of Israel, but in some later Jewish teachings the commandment was modified as distinctions were made between the righteous and the unrighteous. The effects of this change of view were felt most strongly at table where care was taken to discern who should and who should not be served, as well as who should provide the service.[3]

Thus it seems that the disciples in Luke 22 were expressing the ordinary view of the Greeks and of their fellow Jews. It was, after all, a matter of common sense to be concerned to better one's self and one's position in life. It was human nature to aspire to rulership, power, glory, wealth and prestige. In any group someone must excel. What harm is there in asking who it shall be or in hoping it will be me?

It is in the light of this understanding that Jesus' statement is to be understood. The Son of Man, who ushers in the Kingdom of God and is called the Lord of all—he who calls his disciples to preside with him at the Last Judgment of Israel (Luke 22:29-30)—is among them as their servant, as one who waits on table, one who cares for and provides for the needs of others. He is gloriously, redemptively "menial."

Jesus views himself, in fact, as a slave, serving God and God's creation. Jesus thus challenges the common presuppositions of this world, of the Greeks and the Jews, of Russians and Americans, of human nature and of common sense. Indeed, the more one reflects upon the Jesus of the New Testament—apart from modern prejudices and presuppositions—the more revolutionary he seems to be. He is revolutionary in the sense that he stands in sharp opposition to the worldly—and the religious—wisdom of the first and succeeding centuries and demands radical change, change at the very roots of humanity's being.

The meaning of *diakoneō* is not yet exhausted, however. Mark 10:42-45 belongs alongside the Lukan passage. James and John had asked Jesus for places of honor in the Kingdom of Heaven. Jesus denied that their request could be granted. Places of honor were for those who followed in *his way*. The reward of honor was not to be bestowed without evidence of honor. The ten other disciples heard of the incident and were angry with James and John. Jesus then called the disciples to his presence and said:

You know that those who are supposed to rule over the Gentiles lord it over them, and their great men exercise authority over them. But it shall not be so among you; but whoever would be great among you must be your servant (*diakonos*), and whoever would be first among you must be slave (*doulos*) of all. For the Son of man came not to be served but to serve, and to give his life as a ransom (*lutron*, atonement) for many.

Two major points emerge from reflection on this passage:

(1) The way of service is the way of redemption. Service as redemption may be interpreted in terms of the price paid to release us from bondage to sin and death and to assuage the righteous anger of God. Or, it may be viewed as the way that restores us to a life-giving relationship with God by virtue of that turning (*metanoia*, conversion) from the pursuit of greatness (as the world understands greatness) to a life of service rendered to God and our neighbors. The pursuit of greatness, which is possibly the summation of that which constitutes the heart of sin, prevents us from true worship (*leitourgia*, service) of God and thus from sacrificial service towards our neighbors.

(2) Insofar as the Son of man is concerned, service requires sacrifice; it involves suffering and death. To be the "servant of all" (*pantōn diakonos*; Mark 9:35) and the "slave of all" (*pantōn doulos*) is to be so dedicated to caring for others that you are willing to suffer anything, even death, for the sake of others.[4]

The Nature of Service

We have observed how Jesus' own understanding of his vocation as servant extended from *diakonia* as table service, to *diakonia* as loving care for one's neighbors, to *diakonia* as sacrifice. We have also been assuming that this service is applicable to those who would follow Jesus and be his disciples, for in the major passages cited above Jesus left no doubt that his servanthood was for all who would follow him. How are we to understand the nature of the requisite service? What are we expected to do?

Answers are suggested in Matthew 25, where Jesus speaks of the Great Judgment and of *diakonia* as ministering to the basic needs of people. The passage is important enough to quote in full:

When the Son of man comes in his glory, and all the angels with him, then he will sit on his glorious throne. Before him will be gathered all the nations, and he will separate them one from another as a shepherd separates the sheep from the goats, and he will place the sheep at his right hand, but the goats at the left. Then the King will say to those at his right hand, 'Come, O blessed of my Father, inherit the kingdom prepared for you from the foundation of the world; for I was hungry and you gave me food, I was thirsty and you gave me drink, I was a stranger and you welcomed me, I was naked and you clothed me, I was sick and you visited me, I was in prison and you came to me.'

Then the righteous will answer him, 'Lord, when did we see thee hungry and feed thee, or thirsty and give thee drink? And when did we see thee a stranger and welcome thee, or naked and clothe thee? And when did we see thee sick or in prison and visit thee?'

And the King will answer them, 'Truly, I say to you, as you did it to one of the least of these my brethren, you did it to me.'

Then he will say to those at his left hand, 'Depart from me, you cursed, into the eternal fire prepared for the devil and his angels; for I was hungry and you gave me no food, I was thirsty and you gave me no drink, I was a stranger and you did not welcome me, naked and you did not clothe me, sick and in prison and you did not visit me.'

Then they also will answer, 'Lord, when did we see thee hungry or thirsty or a stranger or naked or sick or in prison, and did not minister to thee?'

Then he will answer them, 'Truly, I say to you, as you did it not to one of the least of these, you did it not to me.' And they will go away into eternal punishment, but the righteous into eternal life (Matt. 25:31-46).

To be a disciple of Jesus, to inherit the Kingdom of God and eternal life, is to serve those in need, providing food for the hungry to eat, drink for the thirsty, welcome for the stranger, clothing for the naked, and visiting the sick and those in prison.

This, in Plato's *Gorgias* (517d), is ministering (*diakoneō*) to the body (*sōma*), to bodily needs, but since Jesus refers to visiting the sick and those in prison, we must recognize that ministering includes not only medicine, which Plato calls the true ministry of the body, but that caring or service which involves the whole person. Jesus' teaching is wholistic. His concern is for that wholistic service so vital to human welfare.

From Matthew 25 we learn that ministry or service involves provision of food, drink, clothing and shelter where such is needed, wherever it is needed, whomever it may involve. Such service may be but is not necessarily impulsive. It proceeds from the innermost being of the disciples. It is concerned for the whole beings of people in the communities where they live. It requires knowledge and judgment. Power and justice must always be considered in the rendering of loving service. Politics, science, technology, business, indeed, all of the skills and resources of modern industrial society must be used and thus brought under the sway of the Kingdom of God, serving the needs of whole persons and peoples.

The impulsive shipment of wheat to alleviate the hunger of those suffering in the Southern Sudan may appear to be an impressive act of service. It may be evil if it is a one-time, stop-gap measure, not followed up with such assistance as may help the people there to provide for their needs on a long-term basis. An apparent act of Christian charity can be simply a gratifying ego-trip for the givers, perhaps alleviating their sense of guilt at having an over-abundance of luxurious food.

However, the use of modern worldly wisdom must not ultimately govern the Christian's *diakonia*. Such know-how as we possess is an adjunct to the basic Christian impulse to serve. Without the dominance of that impulse prudence and wisdom may become devices for avoiding the sacrifices necessitated by *diakonia*. Nor must the impulse to serve be made subservient to the gods of the ecclesiastical establishments. We are not really serving people as Christ serves us if we do so in order to add names to the church rolls, or to have something to boast about, or to gain control over others for political, ideological, or personal reasons.

Furthermore, the fact that someone in need is of a different class or race or political persuasion from ourselves does not prevent our ministering to them. Christian service is blind to such distinctions. The point gains force when we remember that our service must be rendered to those in need as to Christ himself. Christ is there in those who hunger and thirst, in those who are naked, sick, or in prison—whoever they may be, even if they be our enemies. The more service is rendered with this insight in mind the more it will conform to true *diakonia* as exemplified by Christ.

There remains the grave danger that we will render service to Christ in those who hunger in order to merit divine approval. True service is not rendered in order that the servant may be praised by either God or neighbor. It is the fruit of our experience of God's service rendered to us through the life, death and resurrection of his Son, and through those neighbors who have represented Christ to us in our need. *Diakonia* at its best is unself-conscious thanksgiving for that divine service.

Here we must recognize the vital importance of openness, of contrition and humility, of such availability as allows God to serve us. To be true servants we must continually pray for the ability to receive the loving care of others with grace and with thanksgiving. As we receive so shall we learn to serve others and to be God's agents and instruments in the world.

George Herbert, in his poem *Love* (III), wrote of the difficulty involved in letting God serve us. He had in mind the marriage feast of Luke 12:37, where the master arrives home from the feast and finds his servants (*douloi*) awake. He girds himself, has them sit at table, and comes to serve (*diakonein*) them himself. The poet also has in mind the end of history, the final judgment, and in particular the Messianic banquet. Thus Herbert wrote:

> *Love bade me welcome: yet my soul drew back,*
> * Guiltie of dust and sinne.*
> *But quick-ey'd Love, observing me grow slack*
> * From my first entrance in,*
> *Drew nearer to me, sweetly questioning,*
> * If I lack'd any thing.*
>
> *A guest, I answer'd, worthy to be here:*
> * Love said, You shall be he.*
> *I the unkinde, ungratefull? Ah my deare,*
> * I cannot look on thee.*
> *Love took my hand, and smiling did reply,*
> * Who made the eyes but I?*
>
> *Truth Lord, but I have marr'd them: let my shame*
> * Go where it doth deserve.*
> *But know you not, sayes Love, who bore the blame?*
> * My deare, then I will serve.*
> *You must sit down, sayes Love, and taste my meat:*
> * So I did sit and eat.*[5]

There are, of course, other reasons for drawing back besides the sense of guilt that afflicted the sensitive Herbert. Others might protest that they were too busy, too self-sufficient, and that giving over the direction of one's life at so crucial a moment was a sign of weakness. Others might simply not be able to believe in or trust Love, the Lord, perhaps suspecting his motives. But all would be involved, as was Herbert, in seeking to retain control of their own lives, shutting out the influence of others, even when that influence was aimed at meeting their most desperate needs.

It is difficult to see how any such persons could be Christ's disciples. The foundation for *diakonia* in anyone's life involves the ability to receive love and service from God and from God's agents in the world. The divine service is perpetually offered to us in Word and Sacraments in that community where people minister to one another's actual needs and to the needs of all their neighbors.

Reference has just been made, not for the first time, to the holy community, the Servant Church. To underscore its importance it helps to recognize that the injunction in Matthew 25 to welcome the stranger and Christ in the stranger concerns community. Jesus may very well have had in mind the Hebrew laws governing hospitality to non-Israelitish sojourners, and the tradition of hospitality maintained by the Semites generally. To welcome the stranger is to serve the basic human need for acceptance and community. Indeed, the fullest development of human potential depends upon that degree of participation in community which nurtures genuine human individuality. Thus the injunction is a far-reaching one, extending from human behavior to human society, and where the latter is concerned we are forced to conclude that any society which will not or cannot welcome the stranger is a sick society and one that is potentially destructive.

Finally, to meet the needs of others, not of the Christian community, we must remember that Jesus is the Bread of Life, as the Gospel of John witnesses (John 6). Word and Sacraments as conveyors of the Bread of Life are for those hungering in the wilderness whoever they may be—not only for the disciples of Jesus. Word and Sacraments as Bread of Life are for the world and in this sense should be taken out of the sanctuary and into the streets. The image of Christ, the Bread of Life, offering himself to assuage the hunger of the human soul, giving himself as the *diakonos*, the *doulos* of all, the good and the bad, the great and the small, the beautiful and the ugly, is the appropriate image, captured most perceptively in our time by the Jewish sculptor, Sir Jacob Epstein. Epstein's Risen Christ and his Christ in Majesty focus attention upon Christ's hands, turned outward in self-offering, the perfect sacrifice for all mankind.[6] The meaning of this gift—the Bread of Life—in and through Word and Sacraments needs to be further pondered, but here we must recognize its importance and realize that *diakonia* involves the offering of the Bread of Life as well as the bread that feeds the body.

Service and Sacrifice

The deepest meaning of *diakonia* is illuminated by John 12:23-26 when Jesus says to his disciples:

> The hour has come for the Son of man to be glorified. Truly, truly, I say to you, unless a grain of wheat falls into the earth and dies, it remains alone; but if it dies, it bears much fruit. He who loves his life loses it, and he who hates his life in this world will keep it for eternal life. If any one serves (*diakoneō*) me, he must follow me; and where I am, there shall my servant (*diakonos*) be also; if any one serves me, the Father will honor him.

The service of which the New Testament speaks is true service when it is entirely focused upon the needs of the other and is unconcerned about the cost in terms of one's own wealth, power, prestige and the like. Indeed, when required, Christian service can cost the lives of those who serve. Martyrdom comes immediately to mind and we should be aware that there have been martyrs—those who witness to God in Christ through the giving of their lives—all throughout the long history of Christianity, from the stoning of Stephen (Acts 7:54-60) to the murder of Janani Luwum at the hands of Idi Amin in 1977. But martyrdom—actual physical death—is not the only way a servant surrenders life for the sake of others. When the Christian life is lived to its fullest it is lived in readiness to surrender all that one has or is in service to God and one's neighbors. The disciples of Christ are people who respect life but are willing to give up all that is life to them if need be for the sake of service. They are prepared to surrender all and to die in such surrender because they have already died to sin and have risen to new life in Christ, life that is eternal, imbuing present existence with value and happiness beyond all human expectations.

The church is thus a people who serve and who through sacrificial service are disciples of Jesus Christ, Son of man and Son of God. This is the clear message of 1 John 3:16-18, where Christian discipleship is defined in terms of sacrificial love. God's love draws forth the response of love.

> By this we know love, that he laid down his life for us, and we ought to lay down our lives for the brethren. But if any one has the world's goods and sees his brother in need, yet closes his heart against him, how does God's love abide in him. Little children, let us not love in word or speech, but in deed and truth.

Further on we read:

> Beloved, let us love one another, for love is of God, and he who loves is born of God and knows God. He who does not love does not know God; for God is love. In this the love of God was manifest among us, that God sent his only Son into the world, so that we might live through him. In this is love, not that we loved God but that he loved us and sent his Son to be the expiation for our sins. Beloved, if God so loved us, we also ought to love one another. No man has ever seen God; if we love one another, God abides in us and his love is perfected in us (1 John 4:7-12).

The Johannine interpretation of the Gospel provides a basis on which to assert that the church is that people for whom Christ died, a people who participate in the divine activity as displayed on the cross, showing forth in deeds of kindness the love which is both their salvation and the salvation of the world.

Furthermore, in Christ as the manifestation of divine love there is revealed the law of human kind. That law, as demonstrated on the cross and in the lives of those who follow in the way of the cross, is sacrifice. As we have already observed, left to ourselves and our own devices we seek greatness in terms of wealth, power and prestige. Service is foreign. Like the Greeks and some Jews we are inclined to identify service with weakness or lack of privilege. Servants are menials. But that is not the final word concerning the human condition. Beyond our innate selfishness—that sin which is the result of our fall from grace—in the very roots of our being as created by God, there is the law of sacrifice, contradicting our selfishness and plaguing our consciences.[7] That law, which constitutes our humanness on the level of creation, has been obscured, twisted, maimed by sin. Christ's sacrificial love recalls us to our *true* nature as revealed in him. Our so-called innate drive for greatness, however it be described, is unnatural.

Christ's manifestation of that sacrificial love which is the foundation of human nature works in us to free us from ignorance and sin, freeing us to obey the law of sacrifice according to the measure of our ability to do so. That is to say that on the natural level of our existence that which is required for the realization of our potential as individuals and communities is sacrificial love (*diakonia*). To live by the law of self-gratification and the world's criteria of greatness is suicidal for both individuals in and of themselves (they end by consuming themselves) and communities (they end by destroying each other).

Two considerations follow.

(1) The church is not world-denying but world-affirming. It affirms, however, that which is life-giving and opposes all that is destructive of life. The church is thus concerned to work with those people and those agencies which affirm life and deny the forces of destruction. It is logically and of necessity always ready to enter into alliances with those who affirm life according to the law of sacrifice, even when those involved refuse Christ and engage in activities that offend Christian sensitivities. The way of sacrificial service often involves the temporary acceptance of that which is otherwise objectionable. This is to recognize the ambiguity of existence between the ages.

(2) The church boldly witnesses to the ultimate authority of Christ's revelation of the true nature of humanity and of the way by which its true being is restored in and through *diakonia*. In so doing it does not deny the revelation of the law of sacrifice in nature and in other religions.[8] It rejoices in the revelation wherever it may be. Its ability to perceive that law functioning in the natural order and in other religions it believes it receives from Christ.[9] To be the church is to see in new and sometimes astounding ways the operating of *diakonia* in seemingly ordinary events.

Writing of the Holy Communion to a certain unidentified "Lady" in 1861, Frederick Denison Maurice, the influential

English theologian, expressed the attitude of one who understands the root meaning of *diakonia*.

> The Sacrifice is His; He gives up His Son for us all. The Son went with the Father fulfilling His will. We can but come, recollecting that perfect Sacrifice, giving God thanks that He is perfectly satisfied with us in His Son, asking to have the Spirit of Sacrifice, and that Spirit, who is within us convincing us of righteousness, of judgment, may dwell in us and quicken us to all the good works which God has prepared for us to walk in.[10]

The sacrificial service of which we speak is Christ's. He represents the very heart of the Trinity and of human nature as created and governed by the Triune God. From Christ comes the motivation and power enabling us to perceive and live by the law of sacrificial service, which is the law of our beings. We are enabled, according to the degree of our openness to receive, our willingness to be turned from selfishness to sacrifice—enabled by God in and through Christ working by the Spirit of Sacrifice. This is for us the Good News.

Service and Liturgy

Thus far we have explored service (*diakonia*) in terms of love (*agapé*) and sacrifice (*hiereuō*). Worship is yet another dimension and one of considerable importance, with various New Testament words and meanings related to *diakonia*.

Diakonia can be understood as any edifying activity in the community, as in Ephesians 4:11 (*ergon diakonias*). It can also be used with reference to the public preaching of the Gospel, as in Acts 6:4 (*diakonia tou logou*). We are quite accustomed to speaking of "worship services"—a redundancy of which we are seldom, if ever, conscious. However, where formal public worship is concerned there are other appropriate words, among which the chief is *leitourgia* (liturgy).

In its early use *leitourgia* referred to such service as is rendered to the state. In the Septuagint (the Greek version of the Old Testament) *leitourgia* refers to such services as are performed by priests and Levites in the Tabernacle and in the Temple (see Numbers 8:22, 25, 18:4, etc.). A comparable usage is found in the New Testament (Luke 1:23 and Hebrews 9). In Acts 13:2 *leitourgia* is applied to the worship of the church, although at the time it still continued to apply to service in the broadest sense of the term. Thus in 2 Corinthians 9, Paul speaks of the Christian duty of beneficence: "God loves a cheerful giver" (vs. 7). To enable the Christian to be generous, God provides him or her with an abundance of good things. Indeed, those who are generous will be enriched in every way. Their generous sharing of that which God has given to them will arouse thanksgivings to God, for the rendering of this service (*diakonia tais leitourgias*)—this generous sharing—not only supplies the wants of the saints but overflows in many thanksgivings (*eucharistiōn*) to God (vss. 11-12).

As Alan Richardson comments: "God's service is not to be narrowly interpreted: it is rendered not only in prayer but in life, in deed as well as in rite: the faithful service of God in public life is 'liturgy' as truly as is the 'divine service' in church. The conception of service implied in such phrases as 'cabinet minister,' 'civil servant' is one of the finest flowers of Christian civilization."[11] This eloquent statement does not go far enough, however.

To *leitourgia* we must add two other words translated as "worship" in English versions of the New Testament. They occur in the account of Jesus' temptation in the wilderness when Satan took Jesus up onto a high mountain and showed him all the kingdoms of earth, promising that if Jesus would only worship him he could have them all. Jesus responded:

Begone, Satan! for it is written,
'You shall worship (*proskynein*) the Lord
your god and him only shall you serve
(*latreuein*)' (Matthew 4:10, with reference to
Deuteronomy 6:13).

Proskynein, used in relation to God, means to bow down, kneel in obeisance, and humble oneself as one would when entering the presence of a great and mighty earthly ruler. *Latreuein*, which came to be the most common Greek word for worship, meant to serve with the service (*diakonia*) of a slave (*doulos*). Such worship is the only suitable offering (*latreia*) one can make to God.[12]

Here we must remember that on the whole the New Testament writers refrain from using cultic words when referring to Christian worship. Such words were too easily misunderstood, having been associated for so long a time with Jewish worship as defined by the Torah. The Christian community possessed no Torah. The attention of the earliest Christians was focused on the person of Christ and his response to God—his service. Christian worship, according to this understanding, involves one's entire existence. As Franklin Young has pointed out:

> Any possibility of a division between 'worship' and 'work' was precluded by the fact that Christ's service was seen in terms of the whole deed of Christ (or God in Christ). Christ's obedience (obeisance) was seen in terms of his total ministry, his words, his deeds, his death, his resurrection, his session at the right hand of God, his coming again. Worship meant responding to that total deed of Christ in one's total existence.[13]

What, then, is the formal worship of Word and Sacraments as we know and experience it through traditional, structured liturgies? Karl Barth is surely right in viewing liturgy, or formal 'divine service,' as the self-conscious event of the people of God as a community, standing apart from the "secularity of its environment in which it is for the most part submerged."[14] In tune with a more Catholic tradition, we might also say that it is in worship that for the most part—by the instrumentality of Word and Sacraments—Christians receive that Gospel which is the revelation of God in Christ and respond to it in prayer which reaches beyond verbal structures into life and action. Or, to put it another way, it is in formal worship that the Holy Spirit brings into being that mutual participation which is the essence of the Christian life.

Christian worship in essence is not a matter of repeating liturgical formulas, praying to and praising a far-distant, impassive deity. Christian worship is the purposeful and fruitful engagement of one life with another, of Christ with the Christian and of Christians with one another in Christ.

Baptism initiates this mutual participation. The Eucharist continues and nurtures it. 1 Corinthians 10:16 is a most important text concerning liturgy and mutual participation.

> The cup of blessing which we bless,
>   is it not a participation (*koinonia*) in
>   the blood of Christ?
> The bread which we break,
>   is it not a participation (*koinonia*) in
>   the body of Christ?

Verse 17 goes on to emphasize this mutual participation as the basis of Christian community:

> Because there is one bread,
>> we who are many are one body,
>> for we all partake (*metexomen*) of the one bread.

Koinonia is the key word here. In John 6:56 the key word is *menein*: "He who eats my flesh and drinks my blood abides (*menei*) in me, and I in him." The point is that the Christian participates in Christ, in Christ's service, and by such participation performs deeds (ministry, *diakonia*) which are Christ's. As we shall find in the next chapter, this concept was of critical importance for Thomas Cranmer and was and is for a full understanding of the *Book of Common Prayer*.

The great goal for the disciple is the life lived in perfect communion (*koinonia*) with God, with others, and finally with oneself in relation to God and others—at all times and in all circumstances. Only one has lived in such perfect communion and that is Christ. By grace we are enabled to participate in Christ and thus to share in that perfect communion for which we yearn.

By grace we are assisted in and through the church—which is Christ's body—so to participate that we are agents of that communion. All of life is meant to be a perfect sacrifice of praise and thanksgiving, which is to say, the full embodiment of sacrificial service (*diakonia*). We are incapable of such sanctity, therefore, as Richard Hooker, the great sixteenth century Anglican divine, said: "to help that imbecillitie and weaknes in us, by meanes whereof we are otherwise of ourselves the least apt to performe unto God so heavenlie service, with such affection of harte, and disposition in the powers of our soules as is requisite"—we have forms of common prayer, prayer books and liturgies of various sorts. Such forms must always be rooted in and reflect their fundamental purpose of enabling that participation in Christ which is the source of all sacrificial service.

Liturgy which sustains people in their weaknesses, prejudices, and sins, is liturgy in need of reform. Liturgy which is all-consumed with rubrical directions and legalistic adherence to so-called proper forms and structures tends—in relation to the underlying purpose—to be counter-productive. The best liturgical practice disturbs the complacent as well as solacing those who suffer. It affects people, instrumental in transforming them from death to life. It is also instrumental in bringing about that mutual participation which is the world's salvation. It sends the faithful out, sending them out sober and joyous, to do the work of the Lord. It is largely unpopular and we resist its power because as sinful beings we have a holy hunger and thirst for God but avoid the change connected with its assuagement. The best liturgy makes change irresistible, excites the reluctant to give up that which cripples them, and empowers us to embrace that which is the source of all hope.

The test of Christian understanding of *leitourgias* comes when an act of human caring is identified as an act of worship and when a liturgical enactment—a worship service—is identified as an act of *diakonia*: when the two merge and are identified as an event in Christ's continuing sacrificial service. Janani Luwum's martyrdom, the prophetic witness of a profound and simple servant of Christ, was itself a Eucharist, for it was a powerful representation of Christ's sacrifice on the Cross, bringing judgment on the oppressors and life-giving inspiration to the oppressed. On the other hand, a simple celebration of the Eucharist in a parish church is an act of *diakonia*—recognized as such by those with eyes to see and ears to hear—for to it there come the servants of Christ to be cleansed, instructed and empowered for a deeper, wider, stonger ministry of service thereafter.

Our problems to a large extent arise from our tendency to separate the inseparable. This is so when we are present at communal worship as mere spectators, not participants, critical of what is happening, of the music, the preaching, the ceremony, and the like. It is so when those genuinely concerned for social action undervalue or deride the corporate worship of the church, claiming that it is escapist or irrelevant. It is so when those who seem to love the liturgy refuse to allow the message and meaning of it to change their lives. Separating the inseparable we endanger the Body of Christ.

Worship is the faith-response of a servant people to God's love shown forth in Christ, the suffering servant, a response in and through the total being to the Christian as an individual and as a participant in the holy community, the congregation of faithful servants.

Service and Ordained Offices

We cannot speak of liturgy without making mention of those offices—those persons set aside for particular functions in the congregation and in the church at large. We speak of bishops, priests and deacons as the ordained ministers of the church to distinguish them from the church's ministry in general.

The vital point for consideration here is expressed in 2 Corinthians 4:1-15, linking Christ's service, with the ordained ministry's service, with the church's service. In verse 1, Paul speaks confidently of the apostolic ministry (*diakonian*)—his ministry and that of his fellow workers—as being not of his own creation but rather originating in "the mercy of God." In verse 5 he expands upon this insistence on the divine origin of the ministry by saying "what we preach is not ourselves but Jesus Christ as Lord, with ourselves as your servants (or slaves; *douloi*) for Jesus' sake." The challenge to the ministry is clear: to serve the church, not necessarily as the church wishes to be served, but to serve the church for Jesus' sake as ones who preach not ourselves "but Jesus as Lord." The truth is plain. The apostolic ministers are servants because Jesus understood his ministry and all ministry in terms of service and himself as Servant. They serve the church because they are served by Christ; they serve the church as servants entering into Christ's sacrificial service for the salvation of humanity. They are obedient to the example of Christ the Servant, witnessing in their preaching to Jesus as the Servant Lord, and suffering with him. To obey and to witness, Paul believes, involves suffering, something one can learn from the Servant Songs of Second Isaiah. As he says in verse 10, the apostolic minister through suffering is "always carrying in the body the death of Jesus, so that the life of Jesus may also be manifested in our bodies." Ministry—all ministry and the ordained ministry in particular —reproduces the life of Christ, a fact witnessed to most dramatically in the martyrdom of Janani Luwum. To live by the law of sacrifice is costly and painful. But as the suffering of Jesus produced life, so the suffering of those who represent Jesus' sufferings in their own sufferings are instruments of life for themselves and for others. So Paul goes on to say: while we live we are always being given up to death for Jesus' sake, so that the life of Jesus may be manifested in our mortal flesh. So

death is at work in us, but life in you" (vss. 11-12). With considerable force Paul joins the life of the apostolic ministry to the life
of Jesus and to the life of the church. He ends saying: "For it is
all for your sake, so that as grace extends to more and more
people it may increase thanksgiving, to the glory of God" (vs. 15).

Those in the ordained offices are called to be dedicated to so
living Christ's life that the whole church is drawn into the way
of salvation through death and itself becomes apostle, presbyter
and deacon, to and for the world of which it is a part. It all
begins with Christ, as Paul insists. A. T. Hanson sums up the
biblical vision of the ministry writing:

> The Servant Messiah carries out his ministry in the lives
> of his ministers. His life is reproduced in their lives, so
> they also are servants. But this ministry is exercised in
> and towards the Church, so as to enable the Church itself
> to carry out the ministry of the Servant. The Messiah
> came as a Servant; his ministers are servants; and the
> Church he created is a Servant-Church.[15]

Subsequently we shall consider the nature of the ordained
ministry, and in particular the diaconate in the Servant
Church, but for now let it suffice to emphasize the proper
relationship of Christ-the Ministry-the Church-the World, all
rooted in Christ who through his service on the cross revealed
God is and is known through sacrificial service, such service as
constitutes the law of our humanity. The whole ministry serves
through participation in Christ's service to bring all people into
the divine life of sacrificial service.

Chapter 3.

The Servant Church
through History

The Early Church

The amazing spread of the Servant Church, beginning from Jerusalem with a little company of Christians, has never ceased to impress observers both in and outside the church. Indeed, the first great expansion was so rapid and so far-reaching that it prompted St. Augustine of Hippo to regard it and the subsequent preservation and growth of the church as one of the strongest proofs of the validity of Christian claims.

Within decades Christianity reached to the ends of the Roman Empire and beyond into Ethiopia in Africa and Mesopotamia and India in the continent of Asia. Such expansion was in part due to the unity of the empire, with its communications and trade routes, together with a common language and a culture stemming from the ancient Greeks. Christianity also benefited from the decline of respect for the traditional gods of the Romans and their dependents, a weakening of inherited religion and moral behavior, and the growth of interest in astrology and in cults which offered salvation through a divinity that died and rose again.

In this situation Christianity offered something desperately needed and succeeded in meeting the need where others failed. J. G. Davies puts it this way:

> With its powerful and coherent structure, its inclusiveness which disregarded barriers of race and class, its fixed principles and at the same time its readiness to adjust itself to current intellectual ideas and popular practices, it spread steadily and surely . . . It supplied the religious hunger; it lifted men from the depths of the moral degradation into which contemporary pagan society had plunged them; it brought assurance of a personal Redeemer who

would liberate them from evil and from death itself; through its exorcists it set people free from demon possession; through its rites of unction and the laying on of hands it cared for the sick; through its closely knit and genuine fellowship it provided a means of community life at a time when society was disintegrating. The religious vitality of its exponents, the nobleness of their lives, the mutual love of its adherents—all made an indelible impression upon those who came into contact with them.[1]

The behavior of the Christian martyrs, sent to their deaths in persecutions at first spasmodic and then general, provided powerful witness to the Gospel. Men and women followed in Christ's way to painful death with a certain faith in the resurrection, a faith reflected by their serenity and their apparent joy. The faithful might say with justice that the church grew because the Servant Christ lived in and through the new community of those dedicated to serving him and others in him.

In essence the early Christians preserved the servant character of the church through sacrifice. St. Augustine of Hippo, the great fourth and fifth century bishop, spoke of sacrifice as the heart of the church, the disciple of Christ being a sacrifice, "in as much as he died to the world so that he may live to God."

This very same thing the Apostle says when he continues and adds: 'And be not conformed to this world; but be reformed in the newness of your mind . . .' (Rom. 12:2). Since, therefore, true sacrifices are works of mercy toward ourselves or toward our neighbors, which are referred to God . . . it is actually brought about that this whole redeemed city, that is to say, the congregation and society of the saints, is offered to God as a universal sacrifice by the High Priest [Christ], who also offered Himself in His passion for us according to the form of a servant, so that we may be the body of such a head.[2]

All of this, St. Augustine teaches, is shown forth "in the sacrament of the altar . . . where it is made clear to her [the church] that she herself is offered in that which she offers."[3]

In that part of the third century Hippolytan Church Order that concerns instruction of catechumens, baptism and the baptismal Eucharist, it is clear that the new Christians are being prepared to enter into Christ's sacrifice and to live out

their lives in sacrificial service. At the outset they must provide
evidence of service performed by them:

> They who are to be set apart for baptism shall be chosen
> after their lives have been examined: whether they have
> lived soberly, whether they have honoured the widows,
> whether they have visited the sick, whether they have
> been active in well-doing. When their sponsors have testi-
> fied that they have done these things, then let them hear
> the Gospel.[4]

After they have been baptized, having divested themselves of
their old clothes in order that they may put on Christ and
having been immersed in water to die with Christ that they may
rise to new life in Christ, they are brought to the bishop, who
lays his hands upon them and prays:

> O Lord God, who hast made them worthy to obtain
> remission of sins through the laver [water] of regener-
> ation of [the] Holy Spirit, send unto them thy grace, that
> they may serve thee according to thy will; for thine is the
> glory, to the Father and the Son, with [the] Holy Spirit in
> the holy Church, both now and world without end. Amen.[5]

The Eucharist follows, at the end of which, the newly baptized
and others having received the bread and the cup, the
congregation is further instructed: "Let each one hasten to do
good works, and to please God and to live aright, devoting
himself to the church, practicing the things he has learned,
advancing in the service of God."

The early Christians certainly knew that they were
"ordained" for *diakonia* and, according to the Hippolytan
Church Order, were to live day and night within the structure
of a holy routine of prayer, ever watchful, having "Christ
always in your minds," imitating Christ at all times, signing
one's forehead with the sign of the Cross, "the sign of his
Passion."[6]

To be a Christian meant to be set apart, to be different, to be
converted from selfishness to service. Justin Martyr, the second
century apologist wrote:

> And we who were filled full of war and slaughter one of
> another, and every kind of evil, have from out of the whole
> earth each changed our weapons of war, our swords into
> ploughshares and our pikes into farming tools, and we
> farm piety, righteousness, the love of man, faith and hope,

which comes from the father Himself through Him who was crucified.[7]

Those converted and baptized into Christ are agents for the conversion of others, working with "patience and gentleness," witnessing through their lives to the sacrificial love that changes people from being Satans to being Christs.[8]

We know now that alongside *diakonia* in the Early Church there was a tendency toward the corruption of the ideal of the Servant Church. Origen, the third century Alexandrian teacher, felt that the growth of Christianity was effecting it adversely—that some entered the church and sought ordination for the sake of gaining prestige and that some when ordained refused to converse with those of inferior social status.[9]

Indeed, the church was changing as it grew. Early dominated by working-class people, it was attracting more and more of the affluent and powerful. This need not have resulted in corruption had it not been accompanied by what Cyprian, Bishop of Carthage in the third century, called "worldliness." Viewing the renewal of persecution in his time, and indeed the beginning of what we call the general persecution of Christians, as a judgment upon their laxity, he spoke of what had happened to the church:

> Individuals were applying themselves to the increase of wealth; and forgetting both what was the conduct of believers under the Apostles and what ought to be their conduct in every age, they with insatiable eagerness for gain devoted themselves to multiplying their possessions. The bishops were wanting in religious devotedness, the ministers in entireness of faith; there was no mercy in works, no discipline in manners.[10]

The reaction to such corruption was to be seen in the increased emphasis on asceticism and the withdrawal of some of the most devout spiritual athletes into the desert. They at first lived separated from the world as hermits. Eventually they formed monastic communities for mutual support, correction and encouragement.

Extreme asceticism could also be destructive of the ideal of the Servant Church. With the conversion of the Emperor Constantine to the faith and the cessation of persecution around 313, the church's position in society was greatly enhanced and what Cyprian described as worldliness grew.

The extreme ascetics became more and more of a problem to the church. In 340 a council of the church meeting at Gangria in Paphlagonia tried to set limits by enacting laws forbidding anyone so to teach that marriage was condemned, gatherings of the church despised, fasting extended to include Sundays, and the like. The council concluded: "We wrote this not to cut off those in the Church of God who wish to practice an ascetic life according to the Scriptures, but those who undertake the profession of asceticism in a spirit of pride against those who live more simply, and are exalted in spirit and introduce novelties contrary to the Scriptures and the rules of the Church."[11]

Clearly, the test was whether or not one practiced a rigorous moral life for one's own sake or for the sake of serving others through participation in the ongoing life of the Servant Christ in the church by the power of the Spirit. In the end the world was not to be rejected but served. It was to be served not by condoning its self-destructive behavior but by leading its people, through example, teaching and preaching, back to their original constitution as creatures of God destined for sacrificial service. This leadership involved prophetic, pastoral and priestly ministries. Concretely it meant all that St. Ambrose, the fourth century Bishop of Milan, implied when he proclaimed that "the wealth of the church is what it spends on the poor."[12]

The Medieval Church

The concept of the church as servant persisted through the Middle Ages of the West. It was in the minds of medieval popes who styled themselves "servant of the servants of God." One of the greatest was Hildebrand, who took the name of Gregory VII. In 1081 he wrote to Hermann, Bishop of Metz, contrasting the holiness of the popes with the corruption of kings. "Kings and princes," he said, "enticed by vain glory, prefer, as has been said, their own things to things spiritual, whereas the bishops of the church, despising vain glory, prefer God's will to earthly things." The pope proceeded to counsel that kings should reject pride and espouse humility. "Let them," he wrote, "carefully retain what God says in the gospel: 'I seek not my own glory;' and 'He who will be first among you shall be the servant of all.' Let them always prefer the honour of God to their own; let them cherish and guard justice by observing the rights of every man; let them not walk in the counsel of the ungodly but, with an assenting heart, always consort with good men."[13]

The aim of a reformist pope such as Gregory VII, and of all leaders of the church, clerical and lay, who were concerned to spread the gospel, was to sanctify the entire society in order that every person should follow in the way of Christ, serving God and one another. The aim was frustrated by many things, not the least being the rejection of humility and the intrusion of pride within the very heart of the church. Popes such as Gregory VII and Innocent III, with their vision of a holy society, were few and the examples of papal venality, corruption and pride contributed to the crisis of the church in the later Middle Ages, with rival popes, kings and councils striving for power over the church, and the rise of sects that tended to identify the church's hierarchy with the antichrist of Revelation. It is difficult—if not impossible—to reconcile the crusades with their violence, greed and the assault on the Eastern Church with the Servant Christ and the ideal of the Servant Church.

That other pillar of medieval society, the religious life of those joined to monastaries and convents, was also a strong advocate of *diakonia*. Cassian, the influential fifth century monastic founder, reported on a conference with an Eastern Abbot in which the goal of monastic life was discussed. The ultimate goal is the Kingdom of Heaven and everlasting life. The immediate goal is purity of heart or holiness. To attain such purity all worldly goods must be surrendered and discipline maintained by fasting, watching, meditating on the Scriptures, and the like. In essence the attention is riveted on the cultivation of holiness which in full flower is perfect charity or love, which is always outgoing, to God and to one's neighbors. For the attainment of personal charity in this world where "inequality prevails," and where "greedy men . . . have seized and kept for their use . . . the goods God created for all in common," works of sacrificial service are necessary. "So long as injustice prevails in the world, works of mercy are needed."[14]

The prime service of the religious—monks and nuns—in community was thus directed toward God. In private meditation and contemplation and in the Opus Dei, the regular order of worship around the clock and through the Christian year, purity of heart was formed and the resulting charity overflowed into the surrounding society where inequality and injustice prevailed, issuing in care for the poor and infirm, in hospitality offered to travelers and strangers, in education, and in other such concrete deeds of service.

We know, however, that the religious orders were far from pure in heart. Their members too often violated the vows taken to maintain poverty, chastity and obedience. And yet the religious life possessed remarkable staying power. During the Middle Ages many reforms occurred, calling the religious back to the ideals expressed by the vows. Cluny, Citeaux and the Grand Chartreuse are prominent examples of reform. And yet the Cistercians, beginning in poverty and simplicity among the reeds and sistels of River Soane at Citeaux in time became prosperous and in need of reform themselves. The more rigorous the order the more wealth and power seemed to accrue to it. Even the radical reform of Francis of Assisi and the Friars Minor fell victim to the deep rooted tendency of humans in society to corrupt the ideal of the Servant Church. Francis, who in his rule led his followers to espouse Lady Poverty, was buried in a great, even luxurious church erected to his honor at Assisi.

The ideal of the Servant Church was to be found in the medieval Mass, the focal point of the church's corporate worship. In the ninth century Amalar, a student of Alcuin in the Frankish court, explained the meaning of the Mass in great detail. To him the liturgy allegorically represented the advent, ministry, passion and death of Christ. The dramatic focus was on Christ's sacrifice on the cross and on the accompanying suffering of the church. The altar was to him and others "the Cross in reference to the mysteries of Christ, it is the altar for burnt offerings in reference to our own self-oblation."[15] What is that self-offering? Both mortification of the flesh (*ascesis*) *and* good works, *diakonia*.

In time the allegorizing of the Mass was carried to extremes —the liturgy became too complex for ordinary folk, participation was discouraged by the multiplication of ceremonies, communion was neglected, and the meaning of the Mass as *diakonia* was obscured. More and more the Mass was viewed as an "epiphany" of God among the faithful. The moment of the epiphany was the center of attention: the consecration of bread and wine by the priest makes Christ present in flesh and blood.

There were those who were keenly sensitive to the changes and the attendant distortions and abuses—including Peter Cantor (d. 1197), John Gerson, Nicholas of Cusa, Martin Luther and Thomas Cranmer. A vivid example of the abuse of the Mass was seen to be the cultivation of the "fruits" of the Mass, what the communicant can expect to gain from the Mass in terms of benefits in this life and hereafter. Masses were multiplied that the benefits might abound. The meaning of Christ's sacrifice in relation to the sacrificial service of God's people was sorrowfully over-shadowed by the zeal for gain.[16]

There is yet another dimension of the medieval church in which the image of the Servant Church is represented. This is that dimension in which Christian spirituality is formed and nourished—the area of popular devotions and of the mystics, great and small.

Catherine of Sienna (1347-1380) was a remarkably powerful woman who labored strenuously for the reform of the church and in the process did not hesitate to criticize the clergy, including popes. She was also a mystic, who in her *Dialogue* recorded the wisdom that came to her from God. Her message was that truth, the supreme truth of God's love for us, fosters love, enabling our ascent to the perfection of love, which is the perfection of our humanity, ourselves as God intends us to be.[17] Catherine recorded the divine disapproval of the wicked, of those who "are set in their way of selfishness, indecency, pride, and avarice, envy that is grounded in their perverse lack of discernment, their impatience, and many other sins." To such God says:

> O blind humanity, to have so lost sight of your dignity! You who were so great have become so small! You who were in command have sold yourselves into servitude to the vilest power there is, for you have become the servants and slaves of sin. You have become nothing, since you become like what you serve, and sin is nothingness.[18]

There are others, such as are most Christians, who are on their way toward becoming faithful servants of God: "They serve me with love rather than that slavish fear which serves only for fear of punishment. But their love is imperfect, for they serve me for their own profit or for the delight and pleasure they find in me."[19] Truly to serve God is to love both God and neighbor.

Indeed, every good of whatever degree comes from God and is made manifest by means of our neighbor. Catherine recorded God saying:

I ask you to love me with the same love with which I loved you. But for me you cannot do this, for I loved you without being loved. Whatever love you have for me you owe me, so you love me not gratuitously but out of duty, while I love you not out of duty but gratuitously. So you cannot give me the kind of love I ask of you. This is why I have put you among your neighbors: so that you can do for them what you cannot do for me—that is, love them without any concern for thanks and without looking for any profit for yourself. And whatever you do for them I will consider done for me.[20]

In fact, we strive so to love and fail. Too often we are distressed when those we love do not return our love or do not love us as much as we love them. The problem is in "the root of spiritual selfishness. This is why I often permit you to form such a love, so that you may come through it to know yourself and your imperfection."[21]

To help the sinner striving to love sacrificially, the medieval church provided the Sacrament of Penance. In a late medieval *Primer* or lay-folk's prayer book in English, there are complete instructions for making confession to a priest, beginning with a rigorous self-examination and proceeding to confession of sins against God and neighbors with the restoration of love through absolution and restitution or satisfaction. The process described is that of turning (*metanoia*) from selfishness to *diakonia*. In the lengthy form of confession provided we find the following:

The seven works of mercy bodily.

Also I have sinned in not fulfilling of the seven works of mercy bodily, by will, power, and deed. I have not clothed the naked. I have not given drink to the thirsty. I have not fed the hungry. I have not visited the prisoners and the sick. I have not departed of my goods to the poor. I have not harbored the harborless. I have not buried the dead, according to the commandments of God. Whereof I cry God mercy.

The seven works of mercy ghostly.

Also I have sinned in not fulfilling the seven works of mercy spiritual. I have not given counsel to them that had need. I have not taught the ignorant. I have not discretely corrected them that had offended. I have not comforted them that have been in heaviness. I have not forgiven them that have misdone or mis-said by me. I have not patiently suffered them that have reproved me. I have not devoutly prayed to God for my neighbor, to give him grace to amend his sinful living, and continue in virtue. Whereof I cry God mercy.[22]

Anglicanism

If, as many say, Anglicanism is best defined by reference to the *Book of Common Prayer* as first devised in sixteenth century England, then it is natural to turn first to the Prayer Book when considering the vision of the Servant Church in Anglicanism. And it is reasonable to consider first the understanding of ministry found there.

According to the Prayer Book and Ordinal, the ministry of the whole church involves *diakonia*, sacrificial service. The child in baptism is meant "to folowe the example of oure saviour Christe, and to be made lyke unto hym"—dying to sin and rising to righteousness.[23] In the catechism preceding confirmation the Christian duty of love of God and neighbor is spelled out in detail. The description of what is involved in one's duty towards one's neighbor begins with: "My duetie towards my neighboure is, to love hym as myself."[24]

In the Ordinal there is a common prayer for all orders, with appropriate variations for each. Here God is called upon to "mercifully beholde these thy servants . . . replenishe them so with the trueth of thy doctrine, and innocencie of lyfe, that, both by word and good example, they may faithfully serve thee . . . to the glory of thy name and profyte of thy congregation."[25] Deacons are ordered to assist the priests in liturgical functions and "to search for the sick, poor, and impotent" that they may be served. Priests are described as messengers, watchmen, pastors and stewards "of the Lord" who are "to teache, to premonishe, to feede, and provide for the Lordes familie."[26] Bishops are to provide an example of good works to others and to show themselves gentle and merciful "for Christs sake, to poor and needy people, and to all strangers destitute of help."[27] On being given a Bible the bishop is exhorted to "bee to the flock of Christ a shepherd, not a wolf, feed them, devour them not, hold up the weak, heal the sick, bind together the broken, bring again the outcasts, seek the lost."[28]

In the intercessory prayer at Holy Communion this particular prayer is made: "and to all thy people give thy heavenly grace, and especially to this congregation here present, that with meek heart and due reverence they may hear and receive thy holy word, truly serving thee in holyness and righteousness all the days of their life." This is followed immediately by prayer for all those "in trouble, sorrow, need, sickness, or any other adversity."[29]

Undergirding such specific statements there was the general intention that the Church of England be reformed for *diakonia*. It was the intention of many in authority that the Church of England as the church of the nation lead in building in England the Godly Kingdom, the *societas Christiana*, which is a society dedicated to *diakonia*. To this end all superstition and every obstacle to full participation in worship whereby personal and public righteousness were advanced was removed or destroyed. Most dramatically, Latin was replaced by the English vernacular. Under Thomas Cranmer's leadership the Mass became the Holy Communion. The altar at the east end was either destroyed or disused, replaced by a table. The table was brought down into the midst of the people at communion time. There the community gathered around—the society visibly assembled, from beggars to wealthy gentry, from yeomen to noblemen. To this company of people the Lord came in the Spirit, came not to change bread but to change people. Thus the consecration came to include the communion of the people, their partaking of the Lord's Body and Blood, becoming more fully his body, sharing in his servanthood.

Great emphasis was placed upon communion—with God and neighbors—necessitating serious attention to preparation for the same through repentance. For the sacrament to be fully what it was intended to be, faithful sinners must be brought to contrition, confession and amendment of life. Having been shriven they were then prepared to eat "the lively food," participate in Christ as he participated in them. They were also prepared to give thanks in godly lives of mutual service and charitable communion, in their homes and in their villages. Word and Sacrament were aimed at the sanctification or mak-

ing holy of individuals and of their communities. The ideal of
the Servant Church was being realized.

It is important to know that the reform took place in England
in the midst of social and economic crisis. Debased coinage,
run-away inflation, the collapse of the cloth trade, and a
growing number of unemployed poor all contributed to the
occurrence of the rebellions of 1549. The so-called Commonwealth Men attacked social abuse and injustice, including the
enclosure of common lands by avaricious landlords, and argued
that all people, rich and poor alike, are mutually dependent
and should live for one another. Such *diakonia* shows forth the
image of God in us. Hugh Latimer, bishop and the preacher of
the Commonwealth Men, excoriated the privileged saying that
the common folk of England "are equal with you. Peers of the
realm must needs be. The poorest ploughman is in Christ equal
with the greatest prince that is. Let them, therefore, have
sufficient to maintain them, and to find them their necessaries."[31]

Preaching was one means of correcting an unjust situation,
the enacting of laws was another, but the most eloquent and
potentially effective was the daily round of worship in the
church, punctuated by regular (although infrequent) cele-
brations of the Holy Communion, at which all of the citizenry
was required to be present. Here in services of worship the
Servant Church was being realized and in the process evil was
being eradicated and godliness, individual and social, was
promoted. Hugh Latimer is known to have been present at
Lambeth when Cranmer was working on the Prayer Book to
revise it, making it more readily an instrument for the reform of
the nation.

Richard Hooker, the sixteenth century English theologian,
defended the English Church and, in Book V of his *Lawes of
Ecclesiastical Polity* (1597), its Prayer Book against the attacks
of the Puritans. He regarded the *Book of Common Prayer* as a
means of perfecting the commonwealth. In it are contained the
public devotions of the society at large. The sacraments are
moral instruments and causes instrumental for participation in
Christ whereby "such effects as being derived from both natures
of Christ . . . are made our own," conveying "a true actual
influence of grace whereby the life which we live according to
godliness is his, and from him we receive those perfections
wherein our eternal happiness consisteth."[32] According to

Hooker, those who participate in Christ not only attain to perfection and happiness, but they do so together, being "coupled every one to Christ their Head and unto every particular person amongst themselves."[33] Participation in the Servant Christ involves mutual participation in the church and in society, such participation as produces mutual caring and help—*diakonia*.

This is the ideal of the Servant Church. That it was not fully realized in sixteenth century England is evident and not surprising. John Jewel, Bishop of Salisbury under Queen Elizabeth I, feared that the reform in England had failed.[34] The aims of the Commonwealth Men were too idealistic and seemed unrealizable, people tended to resist communion, the avaricious were unchanged, abuses and injustices remained and seemingly increased. But the ideal was viewed by persons such as Cranmer, Latimer, Jewel, Hooker and others in subsequent generations as true, grounded in Scripture and the example of the Early Church, and not to be surrendered on account of the perversity of human beings. It is, indeed, arguable that from its beginnings in the sixteenth century Anglicanism has adhered to the ideal of the Servant Church, has sought to cultivate *diakonia*, and has emphasized the necessity of sacrificial service for the church to be the church of Jesus Christ and of none else. The evidence is there in recorded history from the administration of the poor laws in the sixteenth century, to the involvement of our communion in the struggles for racial and sexual equality and justice in the twentieth. But perhaps the most significant evidence is to be found still in parish churches and in local communities around the world where Anglicans attend the Holy Communion and go forth to love and serve the Lord in newness of life, through deeds of active charity.

There remains one additional, important area of concern. This is Anglican spirituality which since the sixteenth century has centered on the sacrifice of Christ on the Cross—the supreme act of *diakonia*. In the preaching and teaching of Cranmer, Jewel, Hooker and others, in the private devotions of Lancelot Andrewes, in the spiritual direction of Evelyn Underhill, and in the poetry of John Donne and George Herbert, and T. S. Eliot as influenced by them, Anglican devotions in the formative years and after centered on Christ on the Cross. Time and time again the faithful were led to meditate upon Christ's passion and to apply it to their lives. Jewel, in a powerful sermon, pictured Christ on the Cross, dwelling on the details of his sufferings, and located the power of Christ's sacrifice now in the Holy Communion wherein the faithful are made one with him and there die with Christ to rise with him, to praise the Lord and to "offer up our bodies a living, pure, holy, and acceptable sacrifice to God."[35] In this deeply felt experience of the divine the faithful are made ready for *diakonia*.

In the nineteenth century Frederick Denison Maurice too meditated on Christ's sacrifice, teaching that through his death Christ revealed the law of human kind. We are social creatures, meant to live in communion with one another, such communion as requires sacrifice, such sacrifice as Christ revealed to us on the Cross. It was Maurice's belief that we should live as people, as societies, by the law of sacrifice—exercising kindness and gentleness—and thus he also believed that competition must give way to cooperation in personal affairs but also in the affairs of nations. This was no idle dream. He wrote:

> The Will that rules the universe, the Will that has triumphed and does triumph, is all expressed and gathered up in *the Lamb that was slain* . . . The principle of sacrifice has been ascertained once and for ever to be *the* principle, the divine principle; that in which God can alone fully manifest His own eternal Being, His inmost character, the order which He has appointed all creatures, voluntarily or involuntarily, to obey.[36]

F. D. Maurice was not the only Anglican in modern times to emphasize sacrifice—and thus *diakonia*. For instance, William Temple, Archbishop of Canterbury during World War II, preached at Repton School in England:

> Think of Him then, the Hero-Redeemer, 'Who for the joy that was set before Him,' the joy of a world won by Him for His Father's Kingdom, 'endured the Cross in scorn of contempt'; hear Him as He pleads with your self-will, obey Him as He calls to sacrifice. In Him, and nowhere else, is the power by which you must serve Him.[37]

For Temple such service involved not only worship directed toward God but intense involvement in the social issues of his day. He spoke of God and His purpose to win society out of "a welter of competing selfishness" into "a fellowship of love." He spoke too of humanity as "self-centered" and yet always carrying in it "abundant proof that this is not the real truth" of human nature. The truth beyond selfishness is that we are made in the image of God—"the image of holiness and love." The image is defaced but still there and capable of response to the divine image in its perfection as shown forth in Jesus Christ.[38] This is the secret of the world's transformation. We *are* servants through participation in the Servant Christ. In him our true nature is restored and empowered.

Evelyn Underhill (1875-1941) was a spiritual director and author of considerable influence in England and in America. She too placed strong emphasis on sacrifice—*diakonia*. Like Maurice and Temple she regarded sacrifice as fundamental to human nature and the Cross as the perfect revelation of it. She spoke of sacrifice in terms of self-abandonment, by adoration and prayer (which is communion with God), living in the "atmosphere of God", abandoned to the working of Spirit. Thus adoration and prayer find fulfillment in cooperation which is divine action in and through the self-abandoned Christian. The action is *diakonia*. In true Anglican fashion she insists on the unity of worship and action. All is connected. Action needs personal piety/personal piety needs action. But there is a certain order:

> First, a personal contact with Eternal Reality, deepening, illuminating and enlarging all of our experience of fact, all our responses to it: that is faith. Next, the fullest possible membership of and duty towards the social organism, a completely rich, various, heroic, self-giving, social life: that is charity.[39]

Anglicanism began in the reform of the Church of England, the restoration of the servant nature of the church. The ideal of the Servant Church has persisted and may be said to be an essential part—if not the very heart—of that which constitutes the Anglican ethos.

The American Past

The understanding of the Church as Servant as it developed in England was espoused by the Episcopal Church in America. By 1789 this church had adopted and adapted the *Book of Common Prayer* and the Ordinal with its provisions for the maintenance of the ministry of bishops, priests and deacons. Service rendered to God and neighbors—*diakonia*—was a

keynote of such official formularies and thus was a keynote of
the Episcopal Church as a part of world-wide Anglicanism.
Futhermore, the works of Cranmer, Jewel and Hooker were
widely read by the clergy in the colonies and in the new nation.
Nor can we ignore the influence of such theologians and
spiritual leaders as Maurice, Temple and Underhill. The
American Episcopal Church has tended to follow the leadership of English church men and women. But there is something
distinctly American about this church, which effects our
understanding of the servant nature of the church.

We may begin with "voluntaryism". Religious freedom, the
separation of church and state, and denominationalism, all
contributed towards the emergence of a kind of church life
dependent on the voluntary support of the laity and thus on
people personally committed. This encouraged democratic
government of the church, from top to bottom, the creation of
checks and balances to limit the power of hierarchies, and a pref-
erence for practical achievement over theological dogmatism.

Evangelical revivalism both contributed toward and served
the developing "voluntaryism". The Great Awakening of the
eighteenth century cut across all colonial and ecclesiastical
boundaries, inculcating democratic, equalitarian ideals. This
was the first of a series of revivals stretching from the
eighteenth century and reaching into the present. It was
inspired by events in Europe and especially the evangelical
revival in England. George Whitfield, the English priest-
evangelist, was especially noteworthy, itinerating through the
colonies, awakening thousands through his preaching. But as
the phenomenon developed it was mightily influenced by the
American situation, the wilderness and the frontier, and the
pressing need to establish a godly order for the new nation.

The revivals were evangelical in their theological insistence on
a conversion experience as the beginning of Christian life. They
were revivals in that they developed a technique to induce
conversion. The Episcopal Church is seldom discussed in relation
to evangelical revivalism. Due to the Prayer Book baptism, catechism, and confirmation it is nurture, not conversion, that is
stressed. But the Episcopal Church did not escape the influence
of revivalism. The Evangelicals in the church became involved in
one way or another and the great high church bishop, John Henry
Hobart of New York, affirmed the evangelical truths of pardon,

justification and eternal life as free gifts of God through the Son by the renovating activity of the Spirit.

In its most direct and simple form what we are thinking of was expressed in the preaching of Devereaux Jarratt (1732-1801), for 38 years the Anglican minister of Bath Parish, Dinwiddie County, in Virginia. He tells of how his preaching brought people to conversion:

> Instead of moral harangues, and advising my hearers in a cool, dispassionate manner, to walk in the *primrose paths* of a *decided, sublime and elevated virtue,* and not to tread in the foul tracts of *disgraceful vice,* I endeavoured to expose, in the most alarming colors, the guilt of sin, the entire depravity of human nature—the awful danger mankind are in by nature and practice . . . These doctrines are very grating and mortifying to the pride of man, and therefore, the more necessary to be often repeated, and warmly inculcated, that the haughtiness of man may be brought down, and his lofty imaginations laid low; that Jesus Christ may be gladly received, as a Saviour in a desperate case.[40]

The quest for repentance (*metanoia*) and conversion can be understood in widely different ways. It can be tempered by humanistic optimism which is also a part of the humanist ethos, it can be influenced by educational theory (see the Seabury Series), by psychology (see the Group Life Movement), and by theological and political realism (as in Neo-Orthodoxy and the teachings of Reinhold Niebuhr), but however it is understood it persists. To be a Christian is to be converted, to change and be changed with manifold practical effects.

Richard S. Emrich, Bishop of Michigan, wrote in the Presiding Bishop's Book for Lent (1945), that conversion, which he views as essential, changes us so that we see the world not as ours but as God's:

> That neighbor of yours, whom perhaps you heartily dislike, is transformed into a brother for whom Christ died, and the trees and the heavens begin to reflect for you the glory of their Creator. No longer do you "stand over against" your neighbor, primarily concerned with your rights. No longer are you just a "jostling ego" in your street. Rather you see yourself from above, one member of a vast world of men for which Christ has a will. And you know that He can only reign if you keep your place, renounce your pretensions,

and set out to reconcile man to man because you yourself are reconciled to God.[41]

From the beginning revivalism has served to create servants and to build up the Servant Church. Samuel Hopkins (1721-1803), a disciple of Jonathan Edwards, taught that the powers of darkness in America could be overcome by "disinterested benevolence." Hopkinsianism held that sin was self-love while holiness was the cultivation of "disinterested benevolence." Self-love leads to the quest for personal happiness at the cost of others' happiness. "Disinterested benevolence" is concerned first with the happiness of others—with the greatest good and happiness of the whole people. In the exercise of "disinterested benevolence" the Christian "will be willing to suffer positive evil, to save others from greater evil, or when necessary to promote and procure a greater overbalancing good for the whole."[42]

One of the fruits of evangelical revivalism and Hopkinsian "disinterested benevolence" was the creation of voluntary societies. They first developed in England, were not tied to any particular church, and were often started by laity. There were three types: those concerned with issues involving public and personal morality, such as slavery, temperance, peace, and prostitution; those concerned with charity, care of orphans and education of the needy; and those concerned with specifically religious matters. Of the latter there were missionary societies, tract and Bible societies, the Sunday School Union, and educational societies for the education and training of clergy. Such largely non-denominational societies influenced the development of societies and departments in particular churches. In 1919 when General Convention created a central organization for the Episcopal Church known as "The Presiding Bishop and Council," it did so by assuming the functions of "societies" such as the Board of Missions of the Domestic and Foreign Missionary Society, the General Board of Religious Education, and the Joint Commission on Social Service.

The concept of *diakonia* in America was further developed by the Social Gospel in the late nineteenth and early twentieth centuries. This movement was a product of the concern for social reform inherent in evangelical revivalism, especially as that appeared after the Civil War, but it was also influenced by religious and theological liberalism. Revivalists such as Charles

Finney were possessed by the vision of a holy nation, a sanctified citizenry, a model for the world. Religious liberals, too, were optimistic. They denied the doctrine of religious sin and asserted that humans possess a natural capacity for *diakonia*. Walter Rauchenbusch (1861-1918) was the theologian of the Social Gospel, teaching that the critical moment in history had arrived, the Kingdom of God was breaking in and was a potent force effecting social reconstruction through the agency of nascent sociology. The aim was to realize love in society in pursuance of Jesus' teaching. Rauchenbusch, unlike some, possessed a strong doctrine of sin, but he was optimistic, reflecting the mood of the time in which he lived.

In the Episcopal Church this teaching, consciously associated with and sometimes modified by the teaching of F. D. Maurice and the experience of Christian Socialism in England, was widely absorbed. Societies came into being such as the Society of Christian Socialists, the Church Socialist League, and the League for Social and Industrial Democracy. General Convention created a joint commission on social service in 1901. Those who adopted the teaching regarded the Servant Church as the instrument for the inbreaking of the Kingdom of God and thus for a radical change in American society, imbuing that society with love, cooperation and sacrificial service.

In 1933, speaking before the Catholic Congress, Julian Hamlin, the rector of the Anglo-Catholic Church of the Advent in Boston, combined Social Gospel insights with the doctrine of the Incarnation, emphasizing humanity in this world: "Every sacrament is for man, to heal him, to restore him, and to make him one with God, and having done that, to make him one with his brethren." Under the influence of the Incarnation the Servant Church condemns injustice, defends the human spirit against the tyranny of machines, and fights for those who starve while others feast. Speaking in the midst of the Great Depression, Hamlin said: "We have blessed bread at the altar, but we have not blessed it in the grain elevators. Every starving man and woman should remind us of that, should make us want to make the Mass more real."[43]

By the time Hamlin spoke in 1933 the Social Gospel movement was virtually strangled—by its unrealizable idealism, its inability to effect a conjunction of righteousness and power, gospel and politics in American society, and by its domination

by the middle class. The first World War and the Great
Depression effectually challenged both the optimism and the
idealism of the leaders of the Social Gospel. Gradually attention
turned toward the personal, the crisis of the self, the crisis of
the family. Kirby Page had taught that "self-sacrifice is just as
natural as any other of man's instincts and under appropriate
circumstances is absolutely supreme in the average person."
But that average person came more and more to doubt his or
her innate goodness, to be aware of the internal struggle
between sin and righteousness as never ceasing and never
victorious, and to lose all confidence and hope. There emerged
in the 1930s and 1940s a new sense of realism, a recognition by
Reinhold Niebuhr and others of the tension between the Gospel
principle of love and the common-sense morality of social life,
and a conviction concerning the necessity of maintaining the
dialectic of Renaissance pretension and Reformation humility.
The Gospel was seen to be a true foolishness.[44]

The mood was well expressed by A. T. Mollegen, professor at
the Virginia Theological Seminary, in lectures given at
Washington Cathedral on Christianity in the secular age. We
are all members of the church and like our Lord have two
natures, divine and human. Unlike our Lord, Mollegen said,
these two natures are not perfectly united in us.

> The worship of the Anglican Communion, because of its
> clarity, shows forth his [Christ's] principle in the great
> celebration of the thanksgiving feast, the Eucharist. It is
> also in the daily worship, Morning and Evening Prayer.
> Whenever our folk meet their God, there is always a con-
> fession of sin—not only our sin as individuals, but our sin
> as a historical Church. And we not only confess our sin as
> a social institution, but we also confess as members of
> corporate groups. We confess the sin of labor, or the sin
> of capital and management; the sin of the white race or of
> the black; the sin of nation, or the sin of a particular
> culture.

> Absolute faith permits us to bear without despair our
> own sinfulness as individuals, as a corporate Church, as
> corporate groups in history. It permits us to bear sinful-
> ness with patience and hope, not by condoning it. Faith
> wages relentless warfare against it in ourselves and in
> our society and in our churches. But we can live despite

our sin because we trust something beyond ourselves; we bear our sin because we are borne by God.[45]

In such words Mollegen describes the Servant Church in modern America, a church of humility and hope, dedicated not to self but to sacrificial service—*diakonia*—confessing that it is much of the time a most unfaithful servant, through repentance becoming more nearly that which it is intended to be.

Chapter 4.

Thoughts Concerning the Vision Now

The Lessons of History

In the last chapter we considered the Servant Church in history. In that very brief and selective review we witnessed, first, the persistence of the Biblical vision of the idea of the church as servant against great odds. In the midst of persecution and in the midst of popular success, the athletes of God— martyrs and monks—witnessed to the reality of Christ as the servant of all, calling all people to sacrifice for the welfare of others. The great bishops and theologians, such as Ambrose of Milan and Augustine of Hippo, spoke and wrote clearly and without compromise of the servant nature of the church. In the early and middle ages the liturgy initiated people into *diakonia* and nurtured them in it. Although the church was not above corruption, in essence it held firmly to the vision. Popes and monastic founders, saints and mystics, followed in the way of the Servant Christ, sometimes against strong opposition, while some among them seemed to become enslaved to egotistic self-advancement and the pursuit of personal power. We have observed how Anglicanism began as a reform movement in England intent upon recalling people to *diakonia* both in their personal lives and in social policies and programs for the benefit of the commonweal. Cranmer's *Book of Common Prayer* can justly be regarded as the instrument for the creation of the godly kingdom—the *societas Christiana*—dedicated to *diakonia*. And we have seen how subsequent Anglicans, such as Maurice, Temple and Underhill, made *diakonia* the center and heart of their teaching. America we have regarded in relation to Evangelical revivalism issuing in personal conversion and social reform, in "disinterested benevolence," voluntary societies of various kinds, the Social Gospel, and much more. Through all of history the vision has persisted. The church in its perfection is Servant—of God and others—which is to say that is has persistently been understood as Christ the Servant present in history.

But we have also learned how fragile that vision is in reality. In the Early Church success which came largely as a result of *diakonia* brought with it the desire for wealth, power and prestige. During the Middle Ages both the papacy and the monastaries were at times so corrupt that the ideals of a Cassian or a Gregory VII were ignored or simply forgotten. In Tudor England the quest for the godly kingdom was frustrated by the avarice of gentry, nobility, and even the Queen herself, and her godly prelates. In America, the ideals of the revivalists and the Social Gospelers were adopted by a very few and were at critical moments rejected.

To some extent it is right to say that such failures of the vision were due to the idealism, the lack of realism, and at times the sheer ignorance of the church's leaders. But it is more truthful to say that the failure was due to the flaw in humanity that we call sin, aptly described as the self's inordinate love of self, which pursued with the whole heart leads to death without hope of resurrection. That the vision of the Servant Church has persisted is due to many things, but two seem paramount: (1) the urge to reform, to recover that which is lost due to sin, which is the way of repentance (*metanoia*) and conversion, the restoration to communion with God and with one's neighbors; and (2) the fact, noted by Maurice, Temple and others in the previous chapter, that the ultimate truth about humanity is that we were all made for sacrificial service and that only through recovery of our servant nature will we find peace and happiness.

Finally, we have learned, especially when considering the demise of the Social Gospel movement in the 1930s and 1940s, that we are *in via* and not yet *in patria*, on the way toward perfect *diakonia* but not there, and that in this life we shall never achieve perfection. We live by the vision, acknowledging our imperfections, our sin. We are repentant sinners, who can edure our situation because, as A. T. Mollegen said, "we are borne by God." Indeed, we can more than endure, we can and do persist in the realization of the vision, by God's help through the working of the Spirit in the Church. With such help we continue in the way of the Lord, the way of sacrificial service.

Rethinking the Church as Servant

It is in the light of such historical perspective that we consider the church's servant nature in our own day. Such consideration involves rethinking the doctrine of the church, which is to reform the church in the light of the Biblical vision.

The first essential truth is that the church *is diakonia*. Secondly, the church *is* people, those people who constitute its community. The church is the whole people of God engaged in the primary ministry of service and this is true because they *are* the body of Christ the Servant.

In order to grasp the full implications of this understanding we must realize that such an approach to a definition of the church stands in opposition to the linear view of the church and its ministry. That view presents a direct line moving from Christ through the Apostles and the ordained ministry of bishops, priests and deacons, to the faithful, the great body of laity. The emphasis in this linear view falls so heavily upon the priesthood mediating between Christ and the laity that at times the church has been defined narrowly in terms of the ordained ministry of bishops, priests and deacons. Such a linear understanding has been a major reason why the movement to realize the "ministry of the laity" has been so frustrated. With the linear view predominating, the center of attention falls upon the priesthood, those through whom the divine power comes to the unordained majority. In such a view the laity is reduced to a dependent and virtually powerless entity. It should also be noted that in such a view the ordained ministers of the church have suffered, having unreasonable expectations put upon them, exercising their power reluctantly, with a sense of guilt due to their self-perceived fallibility, or tyrannically because for one reason or another they choose to believe that they are indeed, "less than God but more than man," being "not men, but clergymen."

The rethinking of the Church as Servant challenges the institutional-hierarchical understanding of the church usually found where the linear view is prevalent. Everything is arranged in such a way that, as in the military, there is a clear arrangement of offices and orders from the top to the bottom. Accordingly, deacons are members of an "inferior order," but they are a step above the laity. Bishops are at the top and are sometimes judged unfairly because they are perceived to be the cap-stones of the earthly ecclesiastical edifice. In this view they are seen as more than ordinary humans and are not permitted ordinary human faults and foibles. And there is a hierarchy among bishops. The Most Reverend is obviously higher on the church totem pole than the Right Reverend, a primate or presiding bishop than a diocesan bishop—to say nothing of coadjutors, assistants and suffragans.

There is no intention here of denying that in this world persons and things are naturally arranged in hierarchical order and that insofar as the administration and jurisdiction of the ecclesiastical institutions is concerned such an hierarchy of responsibility is quite necessary. When hierarchies are governed by diakonia they are not regarded as exercising absolute power over all bodies and souls in this world, but rather they are viewed as serving the purposes for which such hierarchies were initiated, reformed and continued. It is when hierarchies are not governed by diakonia, but rather by the faulty and sometimes corrupt models prevalent in society that they destroy the vision and serve the enemies of mankind, for they then pursue unlimited success to the benefit of their own power and prestige. Jesus' teaching concerning greatness in Luke 22 stands in judgment against hierarchies and hierarchical thinking. Desiderius Erasmus, the great, acerbic Renaissance wit, contrasted with telling effect the pomp and glitter of a papal procession during the age of the Medicis at Rome with Jesus' entry into Jerusalem riding on the foal of an ass.

The image that comes to mind when thinking of the institutional-hierarchical understanding of the church is that of a triangle with the laity on the bottom and the clergy ranked in order reaching up to the pinnacle of earthly power and prestige. During the Middle Ages divine authority and power was believed to descend from Christ to the Pope as the Vicar of Christ, through ranks of archbishops and bishops, priests and deacons, and myriad minor orders, down to the laity. In addition, those adhering to the monastic vows of poverty, chastity, and obedience as hermits or in religious communities were considered to be distinctly superior to the laity. Basically monarchical, such thought encouraged papal pretensions and supported Pope Innocent III in his belief that as the Vicar of Christ he was "set in the midst between man and God . . . less than God but greater than man, judge of all men and judged by none."[1] Toward the end of the Middle Ages, in the age of conciliarism when the papacy was in schism, an ascending theory of government was propounded which assumed that all authority and power was derived from the church as the whole people of God in whom Christ dwelt. This radical reversal of the dominant theory was also hierarchical.

That hierarchical thinking was so prevalent in the Middle Ages is not surprising. The universe was then viewed heirarchically, from the stationary earth at the center, with hell beneath, up through the spinning spheres to the empyrean heaven where God dwelt with the saints. The soul was believed to ascend, as up a ladder, from imperfection to perfection, from impurity to purity, from ignorance to truth, with devils seeking to pull it down and angels seeking to pull it upward. The object was to ascend from earth, and from hell beneath, to the highest heaven there to dwell eternally with God in glory. It was a hard way and precarious. But just as the medieval world view was destroyed with the discovery in the sixteenth and seventeenth centuries that the universe did not circulate around a stationary earth, making it increasingly more difficult for those accepting the findings of the new science to believe that God is "up there" beyond the heavens that we see, so the institutional-hierarchical view of the church was challenged and discredited. Martin Luther and others emphasized the priesthood of all believers, the Thirty-Nine Articles of Religion defined the church not in hierarchical terms but as "a congregation of the faithful" (*coetus fidelium*), Christendom was broken into pieces, pluralism and toleration emerged as fact and necessity, and representative governments developed on the basis of republican and democratic ideals. Indeed, not only was the institutional-hierarchical view of the church, with its linear view of the ministry more and more seen to stand in opposition to the teachings of Jesus, it was clearly outmoded. The polity of the Episcopal Church in the United States was greatly influenced as it was formed by the republican ideals of the founders of this nation. There are carefully constructed checks and balances designed to prevent the assertion of priestly-monarchical powers and the clerical definition of the church. But in spite of the historical developments our understanding tends to be hierarchical. Just as we tend to cling to the outmoded view of the universe, saying, for instance, that the sun is rising in the east, so we cling to the linear view of ministry and the institutional-hierarchical view of the church.

We need to be able to think of the church as *diakonia* and to consider images more suited to that concept than is the triangle (cone or pyramid). One possible image is that of the sphere. The sphere might be conceived of as all known reality. Viewed in relation to *diakonia*, it is all-inclusive (*oikumene*, catholic), with God at the center. God at the center is revealed in Jesus Christ whose *diakonia* constitutes the essential being of all peoples of planet earth, people whose numbers fill up the sphere around the divine center. Holding the sphere together are the attraction of the divine on the one hand and the response of the human on the other. This involves the fullest participation of the human in the divine and the fullest communion amongst the participants— serving God and serving one another. The fact that so many fail to serve as they were meant to serve, that so many struggle against one another for power and privilege, that wars and preparation for wars dominate so many lives, points to the crisis which could end in dissolution if the issue were left to us alone. Permeating the sphere and yet distinct within it are those who consciously acknowledge Christ's sacrifice for them and for all people and seek to follow in Christ's way of sacrificial service. These people are the hope of the world. They participate in Christ's mission to judge, forgive, reclaim and restore the whole creation in the image of God, the divine center of all of life.

The church, then, is a people in the world who are consciously Christ's instruments for service. Those not consciously in the church are also Christ's, for he died for them, and he works through them in various ways without their knowing. Thus, through a stretch of the imagination, we can assert that the sphere is the church, the church actual and potential, actualized as people respond to the call to serve and in time identify that call as coming from God at the center. All people that inhabit the sphere participate in Christ and he in them for Christ is the concrete, personal symbol, sum and end of all humanity, that humanity he came to represent and save, winning it back to the essential law of its being, sacrificial service, *diakonia*.

Among those self-consciously and visibly the church there are various ministries. Three of these have been universally recognized as necessary, although their specific functions have varied down through the ages. These are bishops, priests and deacons. There have been various other ministries recognized as valid, at least for a time, such as prophets in the Early Church and acolytes and others at various times, and members of religious orders from the fourth century to the present. Some of these ministries are gone, some have gone and come again, all have experienced change. And there have been people with healing powers, people with unique ability as teachers, and people ministering as directors of the spiritual life. The Agnes Sanfords, Paul Elmer Mores and Evelyn Underhills of the church have been ministers, practicing *diakonia*, although no bishops laid hands on their heads to ordain them as priests or deacons. In the end one is compelled to admit that given the fact that the church is service we are all of us ministers. Every minister is the object of the ministry of someone else. The fullness of the ministry of the church is not to be found in any one person or order. That fullness is located in the church as a whole and thus we must say that everyone in the church has some kind of ministry by which the church and the world benefit. And this is so because to be in the church is to participate in Christ and thus in Christ's ministry of sacrificial service.

Such thinking is certainly not new. The Roman Catholic Church since Vatican II has been striving for a vision of the church different from the old institutional-hierarchical view, with its paternalism, clericalism, and its immense, bureaucratic, impersonal hierarchy. Yves Congar, the Roman Catholic theologian, speaks not of a sphere when thinking of the church, but of an all-inclusive community, an image that agrees with our spherical one. Within that community there are "the instituted sacramental offices" and various other ministries that exist as "modes of service" designed to be and to do that which constitutes the community. The church is thus first and foremost a ministering community. Viewed in this way the discrete ministries are functional and involve each and every member of the community. Congar quite obviously has the linear view of the ministry in mind and seeks to avoid such a view as puts the ministries of the church between Christ and the faithful. He is also concerned to avoid putting the community of the faithful between the ministries and Christ. His view leans toward the spherical image where the community and the ministries exist in constantly interpenetrating relationships, all *simultaneously* derived from Christ. Such thought conforms well to the image of the Church as Servant (Ministry). Congar puts his own view in this way:

> One can only envisage the ministries as a structuring within a community itself qualified and living as Christian. The ministry does not create the community as if from without and from above. It is established in the community by the Lord in order to raise and construct it. Neither can one say, then, that the ministries emanate from the community, or at least one could not say that without some qualifications; but there is a sense in which not only do the ministries come from the Church, but in the which the ministries are constituted by the Church, represent and personify the community.[3]

It is one of the God-given assets of Anglicanism that such a view seems to come naturally to us and that we find expressions of it in the *Book of Common Prayer* and in the writings of the Anglican divines. In a sermon on Jude 17-21, Richard Hooker first notes that where the mystical body of the church is concerned there is no distinction among members, "all are equally Christ's, and Christ is equally theirs." But, he states, "in the external administration of the church of God, because God is not the author of confusion but of peace, it is necessary that in every congregation there be a distinction, if not of inward dignity, yet of outward degree; so that all are saints, or seem to be saints, and should be as they seem. But are all Apostles? If the whole body were an eye, where were then the hearing? God therefore hath given some to be Apostles, and some Pastors, etcetera for the edification of the body of Christ." And what is the function of the distinct ministry? Clearly it is to build or construct the community, "feeding the flock of God which dependeth upon him, caring for it, 'not by constraint but willingly; not for filthy lucre, but of a ready mind;' not as though he would tyrannize over God's heritage, but as a pattern unto the flock, wisely guiding them."[3] It is, of course, true that we do not always live in accordance with our tradition. Indeed, a part of what reform means for the Episcopal Church has to do with our roots in the sixteenth and seventeenth centuries and the appropriation of such truth as we discover there to be in accord with the Biblical vision and present need.

Rethinking the Ordained Ministry of Bishops, Priests and Deacons

When rethinking the ordained ministry of bishops, priests and deacons in relation to *diakonia* we necessarily begin with Christ's servanthood as represented in and through the whole church. For the ordering of its ministry and thus for the enabling of its life and mission there developed in the church certain offices symbolic of the church's essential character (*diakonia*) and for leadership in service. Bishop Frensdorff, speaking of bishops, priests and deacons, puts it this way:

> Historically these orders, or ordained offices, developed out of the Church's life and mission and through her history they have taken on different shapes and somewhat different meaning, depending on the needs of the Church, in living out its purpose. These "orders" belong to the whole Church, especially in its local manifestations (congregations, dioceses) and persons called to these offices are called *by* the Church and *for* the Church's life and mission.

> We can understand the meaning and purpose of the ordained offices most clearly if we can *connect* them to our understanding of the Church (the body of believers and thus the Body of Christ) as the continuing "sign" of God's active love in the world. The ordained offices have the quality of a sign (and thus are sacramental) because they express the Church's sacramentality—outward and visible sign of inward and spiritual grace.[4]

When we identify the church's essential character in terms of *diakonia* and the offices of episcopacy, priesthood and the diaconate as having developed—and developing still—within the church to symbolize and nurture that essential character it is possible to envision the traditional "ordained" offices of the church in this way, a way which is both personal and reflective of the thought of others and indeed of all that we have been considering in terms of the Scriptures, the tradition and reason:

From earliest times the episcopacy has been regarded as representing and preserving the church's unity, universality, catholicity and apostolicity. That is to say, the bishop exercises *diakonia* when standing within the church he labors to maintain the unity of the church not only in terms of its oneness with all who confess Christ's lordship now, whatever race, nationality, economic status, political creed, denomination and sex distinguishes one from another. The bishop labors to maintain the unity of the church also in terms of its roots in the past—its continuity through all ages—and its destiny and future hope. Episcopacy stands for and labors for both temporal and spatial unity. And it does so to enable the church's realization of its essential *diakonia* with the knowledge that true servanthood is rooted in Christ the Servant and is one as Christ is one, serving to bring all people together in the actualization of the law of the universe—sacrificial love.

It is natural that this basic office should involve oversight of the structures constituting the church as an institution among institutions. As officers of institutions located in different societies around the world, the leadership styles of bishops can be expected to differ widely and to conform to differing leadership expectations. But no matter what the leadership expectations may be, bishops fundamentally function to embody the church's wholeness and to lead their people into an ever deeper realization of that wholeness rooted in Christ the Servant and expressed in all-inclusive *diakonia*—obedient to the law of humankind, the law of sacrificial love. Bishops function within particular institutional structures but fail to realize the essential nature of their ministry unless they rise above the particularities and inspire and enable those committed to their care to likewise rise, realizing the oneness of the church and the world—the *oikumene*.

In the 1979 Prayer Book the bishop is consecrated and made a bishop in God's church as a whole and is to love God and all people, ministering to the needs of the people as seer and overseer. Chief among the many needs is that of reconciliation, communion and unity not only in the church but on earth. The bishop functions to meet this need not only as the representative of the shole people of God, but as teacher, preacher and reconciler, making available holy, enabling gifts that draw people out of isolation and loneliness, selfishness and sin, and into holy, healing fellowship.

Alan Jones writes perceptively of the bishop as martyr:

The bishop in his very person stands for, hopes for, points towards a threatening and terrible universality and all-inclusiveness. It is terrible, at least to those committed to a monochrome view of reality. The narrow minded cannot stomach the pholchromatic splendour of the true *Catholica*.

Here is the heart of the bishop's inherent martyrdom: the call to be a symbol of catholicity, diversity, plurality, in his fragile and broken particularity.[5]

The bishop persists as the functioning symbol of our unity in Christ in the face of apparent impotence to exercise episcopal power in such ways as to overcome the defiance of those who resist community—*oikumene*. Jones cites the Archbishop Helder Camara as saying:

The bishop belongs to all. Let no one be scandalized if I frequent those who are considered unworthy or sinful. Who is not a sinner? . . . Let no one be alarmed if I am seen with compromised and dangerous people, on the left or the right . . . Let no one claim to bind me to a group . . . my door, my heart must be open to everyone, absolutely everyone.[6]

To so represent the universality of Christ and Christ's body the church is challenging and it is costly. It involves sacrifice and at times misunderstanding, suffering and anguish as the bishop seeks to live according to his ideals. No one knows better the need for mutual ministry than does the bishop who is fed by the ministries of those around him, including his family, his people, and his fellow bishops.

Speaking of the order which is generally called "the priesthood," Bishop Frensdorff says that

the *Office of Presbyter*—which developed from the Office of Bishop—"orders" the Church's life of worship and pastoral, caring, nurturing, common life. Thus this office is the sign (living reminder, representation) of the Church's priesthood which is the priesthood of Christ, and means that with Him she offers herself in praise and thanksgiving. This happens first of all through offering of herself in the Holy Eucharist and through its eucharistic life of nurture and mutual caring. So the Presbyter, as representative of the community, is "active" in worship and pastoral leadership, but all (every member) share in *the* priesthood of the Church as the Body of which Jesus is the great high priest.[7]

In terms of our considerations of *diakonia* we can now recognize that the priesthood is instrumental in reminding (*anamnesis*) the congregation of Christians in each place where the presbyter lives and works of Christ's sacrificial death, the sacrifice revealing the law of humankind. Priests also lead the people in the only appropriate response to the sacrifice of Christ, which is self-offering, the offering of "our selves, our souls and bodies, to be a reasonable, holy and living sacrifice unto thee."[8] In so doing the presbyters fulfill the prayer made by the bishop at their ordinations: "May he exalt you, O Lord, in the midst of your people; offer spiritual sacrifices acceptable to you; boldly proclaim the gospel of salvation; and rightly administer the sacraments of the New Covenant. Make him a faithful pastor, a patient teacher, and a wise counsellor. Grant that in all things he may serve without reproach so that your people may be strengthened and your Name glorified in all the world."[9]

Thus, when they are true to the nature of their office, priests are enablers of diakonia. Again, as with the episcopacy, presbyters are involved in various different functions. Most are responsible for administering parish churches, some work in institutions serving the community, others are worker-priests. Furthermore, their specific styles of ministry may differ, depending on personal abilities and on the cultures in which they live and work. Whatever the circumstances as priests they are signs or symbols pointing to the Servant Christ, our great High Priest, and enablers of the priesthood of all believers, which is to say enablers to sacrificial service.

A presbyter is an enabler in the sense that the orchestral conductor enables the various instruments of the symphony orchestra in the performance of the composer's score, providing an effective and beautiful music, such music as inspires and changes those who perform and those who hear the music. The priest enables the church, with all of its various kinds and sorts of people and ministries, to interpret and represent the great drama of salvation, the sacrifice of Christ on the cross, so that both those within and those outside of the church are inspired and changed to live more nearly as they are meant to live, in concert with the law of sacrifice which is the law of human-kind. As we have observed such power operated in the Early Church that the lives of Christians (their diakonia) recommended the faith to sensitive, receptive pagans.

We can speak of the function of the presbyterate in many different ways. One of the most important for our time concerns

the spiritual formation of Christians, that which Richard
Hooker, preaching on Jude, called edification and Epiphanius
procreation.[10] In the present context this would mean that
presbyters assist persons to discover and appropriate forms
and styles of *diakonia* such as are meaningful to the persons
involved and powerful, reaching those not yet involved. The
responsibility weighs heavily upon the church's presbyters.
They too need the ministries of others if they are to do what
they have to do and not be overwhelmed, discouraged, and
depressed by the impossibility of achieving perfect *diakonia*.
We also need to note that the functioning of the ordained priesthood is directly related to the Eucharist—Christ's sacrifice
there represented and the church's self-offering there
enabled—*diakonia* being realized anew. The responsibility is
not theirs alone nor does the outcome depend ultimately on
their strengths and weaknesses.

With our nonhierarchical view of the church we are not
concerned here with the question as to whether the priest
represents Christ or represents the church—or stands within
the church facing first towards Christ and then towards the
laos, the people as a whole. Bishop Frensdorff quotes from an
Eastern Orthodox statement which asserts that the priest, or
presbyter, does not represent anyone:

> He *presents* Christ in the community and actualizes his
> presence in a sacramental way within the body. The
> Christ whose presence is manifested sacramentally in the
> Church is "the one mediator between God and men"
> whose unique, perfect, divine, and eternal priesthood
> —the only priesthood that exists—abides in the Church
> as its own priesthood in him as his body and bride: ". . . a
> chosen race, a royal priesthood, a holy nation, God's own
> people" (1 Peter 2:9).[11]

The presbyterate exists, then, to symbolize and cultivate the
priesthood of the whole people of God, and it is on this basis
that we can refer to the presbyterate as the priesthood. In so
doing the presbyters enable *diakonia*. As the orchestral
conductor is subject to the composer's text (howbeit critically
involved in the interpretation of that text) and functions to
inspire and draw out of the members of the orchestra that
music which effects and changes them as well as their audience,
so the presbyter as priest is fundamentally the servant of God

and of God's people for the sake of the world for which Christ suffered and died.

The diaconate, whether transitional or vocational, is most obviously a ministry of *diakonia*, and yet for that very reason needs the closest and most careful attention. In some ways it has become the least diaconal, in the deepest sense of the term. Transitional deacons have been reluctant deacons, vexed at being forced to spend time—six months to a year or more—in an office to which they have never been committed, which deprives them of a full sacramental ministry and in various ways makes them start out as severely handicapped ministers. Vocational deacons are committed to a ministry of service but sometimes have a very limited understanding of that ministry and too often are misunderstood or even resented by others.

The service for the ordination of deacons makes clear what the office is about. The bishop begins the consecration, praying:

> O God, most merciful Father, we praise you for sending your Son Jesus Christ, who took on himself the form of a servant, and humbled himself, becoming obedient even to death on the cross. We praise you that you have highly exalted him, and made him Lord of all; and that, through him, we know that whoever would be great must be servant of all.

After laying hands on the ordinand's head, the bishop prays:

> Make *him*, O Lord, modest and humble, strong and constant, to observe the discipline of Christ. Let *his* life and teaching so reflect your commandments, that through *him* many may come to know you and love you. As your Son came not to be served but to serve, may this deacon share in Christ's service and come to the unending glory of him who, with you and the Holy Spirit, lives and reigns, one God, for ever and ever.[12]

The deacon, then, participates in and represents the Servanthood of Christ, as should every Christian, but the deacon does so in a deliberate act, recognized by the church, such an act as powerfully effects both the deacon and the church at large. In a report to the Bishop of Massachusetts, this function is described in this way: "This order of servants [the vocational diaconate] would exist to a. *personify* the servant character of the whole Church, b. *sacramentally* represent the servant role of the entire Church to those in need in the world, and c. *enable* servant ministry, especially among the Laity.''[13] In such ways the deacon models *diakonia* for the church.

Such modeling begins with the deacon's liturgical functions and most prominently with the reading or proclamation of the Gospel in the Eucharist. This may not on the surface seem to be a very prominent act, but it is a vitally important liturgical act, the very heart of the ministry of the Word. The deacon is the herald of the Good News that the ultimate truth about God and ourselves is contained in *diakonia* and that in spite of our selfishness, our sin, we can and do participate in Christ's servanthood to the salvation of ourselves and the salvation of others. The proclamation of the Gospel reaches far beyond the reading from one of the four gospels in the liturgy. It reaches beyond formal preaching and beyond the taking of the sacred elements to the sick. The deacon's proclamation of the Gospel is the beginning not the end of the deacon's ministry, for by such proclamation deacons place themselves under the Word of God to speak what they are given to speak, to do what they are given to do, personally to feed the hungry, clothe the naked, welcome the stranger, visit the sick and those in prison, and by words and deeds to model servanthood in the church for the sake of the church and the world. In the renewal of the diaconate during our time we see more clearly the unity of the specifically liturgical and other functions of the deacons. Visiting the sick, which many deacons do, is an extension of the proclamation of the Gospel.

There is another liturgical function of great importance, seldom understood. A rubric attached to Rite I in the 1979 *Book of Common Prayer* indicates that the Prayers of the People are to be led by the "Deacon or other person appointed."[14] As the deacon leads the people into the church and the world with the Gospel so in the intercessions the deacon brings the needs of the church and the world to the congregation and leads them in prayer, prayer which is answered in part as the deacon and the people exercise their *diakonia* as instruments of God serving the needs of the world first in the local community and then beyond. Vocational deacons, who generally are employed outside of the ecclesiastical institution and are by ordination charged to watch out for those in any need, are uniquely qualified to serve as tiding bearers from the world to the church at prayer. Again, the liturgical function extends beyond its beginning in the liturgy. The deacon brings the needs of the church and the world to the congregation and serves to assist and enable the congregation in making appropriate responses to those needs. The deacon is thus one who teaches how to serve, helps organize the congregation for service, and maintains communication links between the church and responsible service organizations in the community. Here, at this point of actual service, the liturgical functions meet: the Gospel meets the needs of the world, to heal and to empower.

Considering the liturgical functions and their extensions there dawns an amazing and wonderful realization that a revived, renewed diaconate could be the instrument of God for the revival and renewal of the Servant Church. It is quite possible that within the economy of God the deacon should be the leader. It could be if the rest of us not only let it be but encourage its happening.

The Value of the Servant Image of the Church

It may be objected that the way of understanding the church presented here is inadequate, that there are other ways equally if not more valuable. There is great profit in imaging the church as the extension of the Incarnation, the people of God, the New Israel, the community of faith, and so on and on. There is more than a little truth in the assertion that there is no one way of imaging the church that does full justice to the mystery of it. As Hooker rightly said: "Whatsoever either men on earth, or the Angels of heaven do know, it is as a drop of that unemptiable fountain of wisdom, which wisdom hath diversely imparted her treasures unto the world."[15] Indeed, as the Venerable Bede put it: "Every day the Church gives birth to the Church."[16] This being so the understanding of the church changes with the passage of time and the change of circumstances. Each new understanding is to be tested in relation to the Word of God and the needs of the world. The Servant Church idea is both rooted in Scripture and meets present needs.[17]

When adhered to the Servant Church idea or image prevents the domination of institutional-hierarchical negative emphases in the church. We are all, whatever our rank or position in the church, first of all servants of the Servant Lord. Service is what really matters. The greatest amongst us must be as one who serves the servants of Christ in revealing that the law of humankind is sacrifice not greed, selfishness, or sin.

The understanding of the Church as Servant conforms to our experience as Christians, for we have grown into the Christian life, into *diakonia*, as we have been served by others. The work of the ministry—the mutual ministry of all Christians and the special ministries of bishops, priests and deacons, nourishes us in faith and *diakonia* so that we begin more and more to attain to "the measure of the stature of the fulness of Christ" (Eph. 4:13). We learn humility from those who have served us with humility; we learn to be compassionate and kind from those who treat us with compassion and kindness (see Col. 3:12f.); and we grow into that state of mind which partakes of Christ "who, though he was in the form of God, did not count equality with God as a thing to be grasped, but emptied himself, taking the form of a servant" (Phil. 2:6-7), because we have known and have been known by disciples of the Lord. This is so because we have been nurtured in the church where the spirit of Christ dwells and works through people.

The Servant Church idea is not a narrow one, but one which provides for the inter-relationship and inter-play of all else. It does not exclude other images of the church, but rather seems to deepen and enliven them and this is so because the servant idea is not only concerned with the person who lived and died for all people, but also because the idea like the person is itself always opening up, self-giving, embracing more and more of meaning in a world threatened by meaninglessness.

The Servant Church idea is fruitful as a basis for arranging personal and institutional priorities. It is unrealistic to say that we will only do those things that are most evidently and forcefully diaconal. We can put *diakonia* first and strive to arrange all other priorities in relation to it. If we self-consciously make *diakonia* the measure for setting priorities we shall discover how many things that we formerly regarded as useless are of value and we shall find that some things formerly regarded as essential are no longer of such great value. It is common knowledge that clergy regard administrative duties as onerous, or at least wearisome duties, but with *diakonia* in mind we may discover to our surprise that administration provides countless pastoral opportunities, bringing both needs and diaconal possibilities to light. On the other hand we may become aware that the energy we are putting into preserving some group with a long history in the parish is not worthwhile, that the group had best be dissolved, or allowed to dissolve itself, while we invest our energies in places where there is greater need and greater possibility for providing service.

The Servant Church idea is ecumenical and fosters ecumenism. It is an idea that all Christians can accept and it focuses on mutual service in the community, encourages the broad unity of persons, is opposed to competition among servants, and depends on the Servant Christ—the Christ depicted in the Gospels, a depiction that none with faith can fail to recognize as true.

The Servant Church idea inspires mission and evangelism. We are not concerned to gain converts so much as to see all people in earth restored to the law of humankind, the law of sacrifice and that involves conversion (*metanoia*). Furthermore, as we have learned, this understanding of the church and mission does not focus upon one means of evangelization over another but rather insists upon the simultaneous witness to Christ the Servant in word and deed, preaching and social service, for we witness through service and testify to our ability to serve by identifying our relationship to our Servant Lord. And there is an urgency involved, for we believe that for the world to be saved from self-destruction all peoples must begin upon the way of Christ which leads from selfishness to sacrifice, from competition to cooperation, from war to ever-lasting peace.

The Servant Church idea overcomes the division between the personal and the social. For to be a servant after the example of Christ is to participate in community for the alleviation of the suffering and deprivation of others. Then too, to participate in community is to find oneself fulfilled. Our well being as individuals depends upon our participation in a common life with others for it is there, in community where our individuality is respected, that we learn to practice *diakonia* and begin to reclaim our essential being as obedient to the law of sacrifice, which is the law of humankind.

The Role of the Servant Church in the World

In 1975 the Doctrine Commission of the Church of England was impressed by the urgency of the global crisis particularly

as expressed in critical problems related to earth's environment, that which Toynbee called the "biosphere,"[18] that which
some scientists and others refer to as the ecosystem. A working
group was established to consider the church's response to the
crisis and a report was prepared, edited by Hugh Montefiore.
That report begins by acknowledging the great technological
achievements of our era.

> People born before powered flight saw men walk on the
> moon. Within five decades medicine moved from leeches
> and cupping to organ transplants. We are seeing the most
> rapid population-growth, and we have seen the greatest
> wars in history. Whole nations have passed from pre-
> literate tribal culture to modern statehood in a generation.
> There are great reserves of adaptability, not only in man
> himself [sic], but in natural ecosystems. But there are
> limits. We have to ask the question, what is the relation of
> man to his own nature, and to external nature? Can the
> natural world and man's own nature stand the strains to
> which both are now being subjected?[19]

The report seeks to deal with such questions. It concludes that
we desperately need to change our attitudes toward ourselves
and our world. We must begin with ourselves, with the adoption
of a different style of living. This change, the report insists,
"can come about only through the agency of a theology, that is
to say, through man's understanding of himself as a creature
who finds his true being in a relationship of love with God and
in cooperation with God in his purposes for the world."[20]
Without using the specific word, it seems that the group is
concerned for the cultivation of *diakonia* not only in the church,
but through the church in the world at large. Indeed, the group
considers that the church as change agent is not optional but
essential for the cultivation of *diakonia* and thus for the
salvation of our ecosystem.

The report sets forth a series of theological affirmations,
beginning:

> To accept God as the Creator of all things implies that
> man's own creative activity should be in cooperation with
> the purposes of the Creator who has made all things good.
> To accept man's sinfulness is to recognize the limitation of
> human goals and the uncertainty of human achievement.
> To accept God as Saviour is to work out our own salvation

in union with him, and so to do our part in restoring and
recreating what by our folly and frailty we have defaced
or destroyed, and in helping to come to birth those good
possibilities of the creation that have not yet been realized.
To 'renounce the world, the flesh and the devil' is to turn
from grasping and greed and to enjoy people and things
for their own sake and not because we possess them. To
accept the Christian doctrine of the Resurrection is to
perservere in spite of setback and disaster, to resist the
temptation to slip into a mood of fatalistic resignation, to
believe that success can be attained through failures and
so to live in hope. To accept God as the Sanctifier of all
things implies a respect for all existence, which is upheld
by his Spirit and instinct with his energy. To accept our
nature as created in God's image and likeness and as
destined to grow toward him involves responsible use of
those godlike powers over the natural environment which
God has put in our hands.[21]

Such affirmations reflect a radical change of attitudes—the
change needed if society is to deal creatively with the crises
plaguing it. It is a change that "could eventually bring an end to
the promotion of collective envy, greed and covetousness which
influence all sections of a modern consumer society. In their
place we would cultivate the less spectacular but essential
virtues of equity, temperance, thrift, and generosity."[22]

The Servant Church has a clear mandate to preach the
Gospel and to cultivate diakonia. How shall the church do this?
First of all in the ways it has been empowered to do it, through
preaching and teaching, through the ministry of the sacraments
and the sacramental ministry, through training and discipline,
and through that mutual caring that congregational life
inspires. Secondly, it shall do it by responding positively to
such need as is expressed in the craving for spirituality, but
responding in such ways that greater egoism or mere pious
sentimentality are not encouraged, but rather sacrificial
service, diakonia. Thirdly, it shall do it by setting an example,
modeling that style of life, that community and communion, that
is the hope of the world. Becoming in action that which it is in
essence those outside the church will see the possibilities for
the future in much the same way that pagans in antiquity saw
and were impressed by the quality of life, the love and caring
that they found in the followers of Christ.

Clearly, as the report discussed above suggests, the first imperative concerns the change of attitudes and thus of life styles. Involved in such change is the cultivation of caring attitudes towards the victims of envy, greed and covetousness —and toward all that suffer for whatever causes. The Christian servant reaches out with compassion to the hungry, the naked, the sick and troubled, the lonely and those in prison, the oppressed and those undergoing societal rejection of any sort, including racial and sexual discrimination. There are more ways of serving such persons in need than can be mentioned here. What matters is the servant's attitudes towards those in need, the willingness and ability to perceive Christ there in the needful calling us to serve with the service with which he serves us.

There is no denying that at times we shall turn away, offended by the looks or the smells of the poor, the decay of the chronically ill and the elderly, the language, fear and hate of the imprisoned or oppressed. It is then that we need to confess our sin, accept forgiveness, and strive for newness of life, acknowledging how God so loved us that he gave his only Son for us, for us with all our imperfections, our faults, our sins. Having done that we are ready to minister as we are able and directed to minister—recognizing our limits and handicaps, seeking the assistance of others as we become aware of our needs. Some may feel that they are wasting their time caring for others in their particular distress—that there are more important things to be done. Some may feel overwhelmed when standing in the midst of a great city, knowing that there are multitudes suffering and in need. Then, again, we need to confess our sin, acknowledging out finitude, accepting forgiveness, realistically assessing our ability, alone and in community, doing what we can with the time and opportunities God has provided for us. "If anyone has the world's goods and sees his brother [or sister] in need, yet closes his heart against him, how does God abide in him?" (1 John 3:16).

What this means for the Servant Church as a whole is that in its corporate life it responds concretely to the summary of the law, loving God and loving one's neighbours. Reflecting on the meaning of Matthew 25 can be helpful in determining what specifically the role of the Servant Church in the world should be.

To feed the hungry and to provide for those who thirst means, on the physical plane, that as a church we seek to overcome poverty and in the meanwhile provide food and drink for the critically needful. It also means that we are concerned as human beings and Christians over the growth of hunger in the world and the growing shortage of clean water around the globe[23]—so concerned that as a church we take initiative, together with any others thus concerned, to see that all of our technological skills are applied to the solution of such problems and that our people and the rest of the earth's people recognize the problem and adopt attitudes that encourage moderation, temperance and self-sacrifice. On the spiritual plane it means to provide bread of life and the water of life (John 6-7) to all in need through kerygma (proclamation) and didache (teaching), whereby people grow into Christ, claiming full stature as sacrificial servants, imbued with those attitudes needed to feed the hungry and to provide drink for those who thirst.

To welcome the stranger means on the physical plane welcoming not only refugees such as the boat people of Cambodia, but also any who come into our communities including drifters and runaways. Welcoming involves helping them constructively and imaginatively and not simply making some gesture or saying hello. Here we are concerned, too, with any whose previous inter-relationships have broken down or been destroyed and who are reaching out for new relationships, such as the bereaved and especially now the divorced and their dependents.[24] On the spiritual level welcoming has to do with recognizing and dealing with loneliness in modern society, in the cities and in remote rural areas, in suburbia and in exurbia. Loneliness does not know distinctions between city and country, rich and poor, married and unmarried. To recognize and deal with loneliness involves building the community of faith so that in relation with God and with one another we never need feel that no one cares for us or watches over our needs. Christians are community builders.

To clothe the naked on the physical plane concerns providing adequate clothing for those in need of such, but it also involves the provision of adequate housing as protection against the violence of weather and as assurance of private space in which to develop as whole persons and to be community builders. Our concern reaches from the homeless who need some shelter on cold winter nights, to the elderly and low income groups who need adequate housing, to the education of middle-class and wealthy citizens, preparing them for the kind of clothing and housing appropriate to caring Christians in an age of growing scarcity. On the spiritual plane this concerns putting on Christ (Rom. 13, Gal. 3, Eph. 4, Col. 3), dying to self and rising to newness of life in Christ so that we become daily more like him in his compassionate service to us and to all people. In him we are sheltered from enslavement to evil and are armed to do battle with the forces of evil (Eph. 6:16). Thus we are temples (houses) of the living God in whom the Spirit lives, the Spirit of sacrificial service (1 Cor. 3:16, 2 Cor. 6:16). To realize that we are thus clothed and are such houses is to adopt the attitude necessary for entry into the future with hope.

To visit the sick is to care for them, to seek them out wherever they may be and to provide as best we can for their spiritual and physical needs. On the physical plane it means providing for the care and healing of those suffering from physical or mental distress, seeing that our communities have adequate facilities in hospitals and other caring agencies to meet their needs. In doing this we do our best as God directs us, doctoring, nursing, providing chaplaincies, nursing aides, social workers, dieticians, janitors and administrators. Where the community is slack in providing essential care the congregation of Christian servants may very well take initiative founding and managing nursing homes, hospices, agencies for dealing with alcohol and drug addiction. For a long time now Christians have told themselves that local, state and federal governments have taken over responsibility for health care and that the church need not be involved as once it was except for the provision of "religious" services, but recent events have shown that nursing homes run as business ventures are too often corrupt and that the public and private sectors are not prepared to care for the increasing numbers of elderly persons in our society. A New York State legislator, after the gross corruption of one nursing home operator was exposed, pled with the churches to get back into health care in a serious way. On the spiritual plane our caring is expressed in prayer, in spiritual counsel, in healing, in the provision of the sacraments. Here we recognize the wisdom of the wholistic health movement and the fact that people physically or mentally ill suffer spiritually, are sinners as we all are, standing in need of forgiveness and the strength of spirit that comes with knowing that God loves them. The sickness of the soul is a primary concern of Christian servants.

To visit those in prison is to express concern for those incarcerated in our penal institutions, but it is also to participate in their rehabilitation through chaplaincies, through volunteer work of various kinds, through lobbying in legislatures for the money and talents needed, through providing in our communities half-way houses which assist prisoners in making a successful re-entry into society. Rehabilitation is often criticized. We would rather keep those convicted of crimes behind bars. The criticism is most acute when an ex-prisoner commits another crime and seems to put the lie to the rehabilitation program through which he or she went. The fault may lie with the lack of community involvement. Caring for those in prison in our time may mean that Christian servants become personally involved in defending, perfecting, funding and overseeing rehabilitation efforts in prisons and in their own communities. By extension of meaning here we can justly consider that to visit those in prison is to take action for the restoration or liberation of all those whose lives are limited because of some aberration or some lack. Christian servants are concerned to provide freedom for the handicapped and the disabled, they are concerned to liberate people from enslavement to their prejudices and to all that cuts off one person from relationship with another. They are concerned, too, to liberate people from enslavement to ignorance. Christian servants are mightily concerned for education, such education as humanizes people, enlarging and enriching their lives. They are concerned for liberation from poverty, from tyranny, and from all that diminishes human existence in the sight of God. On the spiritual plane, Karl Barth puts it best. For the great Swiss theological liberation involved transformation from an old and dying being to a new and saving being. Thus transformed Christians are "the image and analogy of the great and perfect transition, namely of the liberation of the world and all men [humanity] which God accomplished in Jesus Christ." Barth believed that thus liberated Christians acquire their "share in the grace of God addressed to the world" and all of its inhabitants, "being personally qualified for that which" makes them Christians, "that is for service as witnesses of Jesus Christ."[25]

If we meditate thus on Matthew 25 in relation to perceived need in our time, we would do well to consider (1) that the physical and the spiritual are separated only for the purpose of analysis and that Christian thinking is wholistic, Incarnational, and, in William Temple's way of putting it, "materialistic." (2) We should not meditate alone interpreting the calls we hear as though they are to us alone. We must remember that we participate in the church and thus, although we cannot even begin to do everything that needs doing, we are involved in everything that is done through the church. (3) Being servants means paying attention to the structures that effect our lives and the lives of all people. Being servants in our time means being political in the sense that we direct attention to effecting changes in the structures of society that they may serve people better and not enslave or destroy them.[26] (4) Being a servant now means being realistic, making hard choices, knowing that whatever we do that is good is marred by sin. Thus we may have to choose between persons or causes that on the surface are equally needful, or we may have to deny a call for help knowing that the help requested is destructive and not saving.[27] (5) We are basically change agents, concerned to alter basic attitudes toward self and towards the world. We're all involved in this servanthood, a servanthood that is costly, frustrating and at times capable of driving saints to anxiety and fear. Then we need to remember that as we have died with Christ so we have risen with him. We participate in that which is ultimate, is life not death, and is the way of faith, hope and love.

With all of this in mind we turn now to consider some of the things happening in the Episcopal Church now that conform to the image of the church as servant.

Chapter 5.

Realizing the Vision
The Diaconate and the Church

Diakonia and the Diaconate

As was said at the outset, this study was generated out of the concern of the Bishops of the Episcopal Church, and other persons, for the future of the order of deacons—especially the permanent or vocational diaconate—and for some reconsideration of the diaconal nature of the whole church—all denominations and all orders, including the laity.

In the foregoing chapters we have taken note the church's situation in the world today and it has been suggested that present needs demand that cultivation of sacrificial service (*diakonia*) which is essential to the church's being. We have examined the biblical basis for the diaconal nature of the church and the relation of that foundation to the church's worship (it is essentially diaconal) and ministry. It is clear that the church and all of its members exercise ministries of *diakonia* and that the particular orders must be viewed in the light of that fact. We then, quite briefly, and some may justly say superficially, reviewed the history of the church in terms of *diakonia* and in the process observed the importance of sacrificial service in Anglican tradition. Finally, some suggestions about rethinking the church as *diakonia* were presented. The mutuality of ministry was emphasized, hierarchical thinking was challenged, a nonhierarchical (spherical) way of imaging the church was considered, the three orders of bishop, priest and deacon were reviewed in relation to *diakonia*, the value of the servant image considered and the role of the servant church in the world viewed once more. The chapter ended where the first chapter started. The Servant Church simply being what it is ministers to the needs of the world.

But what of the diaconate? Questions persist. In particular those dedicated to the cultivation of the ministry of the laity and to mutual ministry question the necessity of the vocational diaconate and fear that its renewal will inhibit the realization of the ministry of the whole church. This study has suggested, time and time again, that before considering any particular ministry it is necessary to consider the ministry of the whole church in all of its amazing variety. It is requisite, before all else, to recognize the extension of Christ's ministry of sacrificial service through the worship, through and work of Christ's body, the church. Then, and only then, can we properly assess the roles of bishops, priests and deacons. In this light it was suggested in the last chapter that vocational deacons are called upon to "*personify* the servant character of the entire church," to "*sacramentally* represent the servant role of the entire church to those in need in the world," and to "*enable* servant ministry, especially among the laity." Viewed thus, deacons have a special responsibility to cultivate lay ministry and mutual ministry.

Now, it is time to consider some of the arguments for the diaconate in the light of the diaconal nature of the church.

The Historical Argument

At the outset we are confronted by the Preface to the Ordinal. Based on the preface to the Ordinal of 1550 it begins, in the 1979 Prayer Book:

> The Holy Scriptures and ancient Christian writers make it clear that from the apostles' time, there have been different ministries within the church. In particular, since the time of the New Testament, three distinct orders of ordained ministers have been characteristic of Christ's holy catholic Church.

Bishops and priests are named, and then deacons:

> who assist bishops and priests in all of this work [the work of leading, governing, and uniting and of evangelization and pastoral care, preaching and the administration of sacraments]. It is also a special responsibility of deacons to minister in Christ's name to the poor, the sick, the suffering, and the helpless.[1]

And thus, Massey Shepherd comments: "However much scholars may dispute the origins and primitive significance of the threefold Orders of Ministry of the historic Church, there can be no debate respecting their existence in the time of the apostles."[2]

Furthermore, it should be noted that our reference is not to a token order of deacons and not simply to a transitional diaconate, but to a *permanent order*. Therefore the Roman Catholic Church from the time of Second Vatican Council, has viewed the establishment of a permanent diaconate as a restoration that rectifies a lack within the ordained ministries of the church.[3]

The task is the acknowledgment of *diakonia* as essential to the church's mission and its order. The history of the diaconate demonstrates how that order was seen as mirroring Jesus Christ as Servant. Through the first four centuries the diaconate was accepted as a vital part of the church's total ministry. Up to the Council of Nicea (325) the diaconate enjoyed its Golden Age: deacons were deacons, serving under and at the direction of bishops, dedicated to works of charity, with special responsibilities in relation to the worship of the church. From then on the order was in decline, in large part because of the development of a sacerdotal, omnivorous priesthood and in part because many of its functions were assumed by active religious orders of women and men. By the twelfth century the order was markedly different from what it had been in its Golden Age. The role of the deacon had changed: "once the associate of the bishop, now an assistant to the priest; once a minister of charity, now a mere 'waiter at tables'; once a minister of worship, now a ceremonial appendage."[4] As the medieval Peter Cantor said, the deacon was simply a "secretary at the altar."

The restoration of the diaconate in a time when the church and the world desperately need *diakonia* seems reasonable— and Anglican. Richard Hooker, at the outset of Book V of the *Lawes of Ecclesiastical Polity*, asserted: "Neither may we . . . lightlie esteeme what hath bene allowed as fitt in the judgment of antiquitie and by longe continewed practise of the whole Church, from which unnecessarilie to swarve experience hath never as yet found it safe" (V.7.4). Quite obviously, Hooker did not advise retaining that pertaining to the outward serviceable worship of the church simply because it was ancient and had long been continued in use. He did demand respect for such things and would argue that where anything is either ordered

by divine precept or is reasonable (generally effectual in setting
forth godliness) and necessary in the judgment of the church,
being done with equity—it is to be restored if corrupted and
disused. In this sense the reformation and renewal of the church
in this age is in part at least related to the restoration of the
diaconate as a permanent order with authority in terms of
service defined as *diakonia* and *litourgia*.

The Symbolic Significance of the Diaconate

A symbol differs from a sign in that a sign is not organically
or necessarily rooted in that to which it points and can be
changed as needed. A symbol participates in that for which it
stands and "grows and dies according to the correlation between that which is symbolized and the persons who receive it
as a symbol." It cannot be changed without enormous disruption
and destruction. Symbols are thus "double-edged. They are
directed toward the infinite which they symbolize"—in which
they participate—"and toward the finite through which they
symbolize it. They force the infinite down to finitude and the
finite up to infinity. They open the divine for the human and the
human for the divine."[5]
The deacon is the enfleshment of that *diakonia* which is
properly Christ's and constitutes the very being of the church.
As such the deacon is a living symbol, a profoundly religious
symbol and not just a sign, because the deacon participates as
a deacon in that for which he or she stands and represents it to
and for the church and the world. Simply by being a deacon,
the deacon is a symbol to the church and the world, bringing
judgment upon all that runs contrary to *diakonia* and reminding,
encouraging, enabling *diakonia* in the church and the world.
The deacon as a symbol is powerful or weak according to the
degree to which he or she participates in the *diakonia* which is
at the heart of the universe and thus, however imperfectly,
mirrors or images Jesus Christ, the sacrificial Servant. To
participate in that which the diaconate symbolizes is no passive
occupation. Participation brings involvement in the servant
ministry of Christ in the world. It requires the turning of the
deacon from selfishness to sacrifice, not just once but over and
over again. Some might refer to the necessary destruction of
the self with all of its sinfulness, but I would prefer to think of

the deacon becoming more and more fully human with the increasing appropriation of sacrificial service. Such service is, as has been said more than once along the way, the law of human kind revealed in the sacrifice of Christ, for us and for all people in earth. To be a deacon is to become more fully human and thus more fully the instrument of the divine. The way of self-denial (denial of selfishness) is the way of self-fulfillment (the affirmation of the ultimate value of life lived for others).

There is, however, another side to this consideration. The symbol must be accepted as such. It is still a symbol, whether accepted or not, but the deacon is a symbol for a purpose and that purpose involves the enabling of sacrificial service in all of the church and, ultimately, in all of the world. And thus we can say that the deacon as symbol is either powerful or weak to the degree that he or she is perceived as imaging the Servant Christ and enabling sacrificial service. A deacon may be as nearly that which he or she is meant to be, but if the people around the deacon are not open, wrongly perceive the symbol, or distort it, the deacon's symbolic value or witness is diminished if not destroyed.

This is not the whole story, however. In most cases there is a mixture of reactions to the deacon as symbol, with some who perceive and some who are blind to the symbol's meaning and power. But even if in a given situation all seem to be blind to the witness of the symbol, the symbol has its effect, working judgment, conveying grace, for the symbol participates in that for which it stands and is thus never wholly without effect, no matter how difficult it is to see positive effects. This is not easily understood by those in our society who are accustomed to judging people and things in terms of immediately discernible effects, effects that contribute to equally discernible gains for ourselves and our society. Most of the time, it would seem, the diaconate has mixed effects, there is ambiguity in the results of its witness and work, and no one knows this better than the conscientious deacon who knows the difficulties of realizing the vision of servanthood not only in the church and the world around but deep inside. There is ambiguity within and there is tension between the call to live for others and the need to be protective of the self.

If we in our society fail to appreciate the diaconate without evidence of actual, positive effects, we are also prone to reject the tension involved in the working of the symbol. The tension to which I refer is fundamentally that between the infinite and the finite, the divine and the human. The tension is there in the deacon who as symbol participates in the infinite and represents the infinite in finite forms as a human being. The tension is there between the deacon as symbol and those for whom the deacon is symbol—the people of God, bishops and priests as well as laity. There is suffering inherent in such tension. For this reason the church needs to provide pastoral care for deacons as well as expecting pastoral care from deacons. Mutual ministry is one way of regarding what is needed. But beyond the suffering there is joyous revelation. For those available to such revelation the diaconate brings heaven to earth, images the fundamental law of humankind, which is the law of sacrificial love, and enables the realization of *diakonia* in personal and social existence.

The Diaconate:
A Bridge between Laity and Presbyters/Bishops

One matter that most concerns a large number of people is that the promotion of the vocational diaconate seems to further clericalize the church and detracts from emphasis upon the ministry of the laity and mutual ministry, which tends to emphasize the laity. This need not be the case.

One Roman Catholic author regards the permanent diaconate potentially as "a great vehicle of 'declericalization' of ministry."

Deacons are canonically clerics, but they do not dress like clerics, they are not addressed as clerics, they are not celebates as clerics have been, they keep their secular jobs as clerics do not. They demonstrate, then, that 'ordination' does not have to mean entrance into a class or caste visibly distinct from the rest of the Church. Deacons, then, can give a different vision of what 'ordained ministry' means which, in due time, will undoubtedly have its effect upon other groups of ministers.[6]

The Episcopal Church does not require celibacy of its ordained ministers, but in other respects the vocational diaconate *could* be distinguished from the other clergy as they are in the Roman Catholic Church, and thus be more closely associated with the laity. This is especially true where dress and address are concerned. There are many worker-priests, but they are a distinct minority while vocational deacons are customarily employed in work outside the institutional church, in the work-a-day world where the laity live out a significant part of their lives. Dress, address and secular employment are not the ultimate matters, of course. They serve the greater cause by emphasizing that the diaconate is not *above* the laity but is *of* the laity, serving to cultivate the servant ministry of the whole church.

As has been suggested, deacons bridge clerical and lay ministries. When deacons read the Gospel and from time to time preach the Word, they do so as ordained persons, canonically authorized. When deacons lead the people in intercessions they do so as laity, speaking out of the midst of the *laos*. When they read the Gospel they do so on the basis of education and training, the study of the Scripture, theology, history, liturgics, ethics and pastoral theology—the theological education designed for leadership in the church. When they lead intercessions they do so with all such education and training in mind but most importantly they do so as people whose regular employment is no different from the employment of other laity. And thus, whether reading the Gospel or leading the intercessions they bridge the gap dividing theologically highly educated and trained clerics and those of the laity with education and skills quite different but equally as important to the life of the church.

If everyone involved—laity, priests and bishops, and deacons too—were able to obtain such a perspective on the diaconate, we should be able to anticipate exciting and positive results. The ministry of the laity would benefit through the example of deacons working "in the world" as laity while associated with priests and bishops in their ordained ministries. A renewed diaconate *can* be an agent for "declericalization," as has been said, an order of persons respected as participants in the ordained ministry with the status and perspective of the laity. Bridging the gap, they challenge the dominance of priests in the servant ministry of the church and demonstrate the values of a non-professional worker-cleric for the mission of the church.

Ultimately, the recovery and development of the servant ministry of the entire church is the goal for which we strive. The vocational diaconate can serve to meet that goal. Work toward that end is first of all a matter of vision and perspective. At the moment, if the diaconate is to be a helpful bridge between the laity and the ordained priests and bishops of the church, it would be in order to give some thought to the declericalization of this order and the strengthening of its ties to the laity. Such thought would probably suggest various ways and means of accomplishing this, some have already been talked about in the church and we have the examples of other churches. The most promising discussion should start with the deacons themselves.

Some Practical Considerations

The vocational diaconate can help to serve some of the practical needs of the church. The renewal of the diaconate in the Roman Catholic Church was inspired in part by the recognition at the Second Vatican Council that in some mission areas there were people functioning as deacons—"preaching the Word of God as catechists, governing scattered Christian communities in the name of the bishop or parish priests, or exercising charity in the performance of social and charitable works."[7] They became deacons before being ordained deacons because things long associated with the order of deacons were demanded by circumstances. In a similar way there have been places in the Episcopal Church, and in world-wide Anglicanism, where certain laity have been called forth and trained to meet pressing needs: in Alaska, where widely separated missions could not adequately be serviced by the bishop or priests; in Michigan during the 1950s when mission churches were being built at an astounding rate and licensed lay readers were trained at the newly founded diocesan school; and elsewhere where responsible leadership was needed to meet actual needs. They were not called deacons for the diaconate was almost wholly associated with a transitional stage for those on their way into the priesthood. There were deaconesses, of course, women who served valiantly, running church institutions, from nursing homes to parishes, ministering to the sick and the poor, serving under the direction of a bishop or priest, preserving the ideal of the diaconate by actually being deacons. The renewal of the diaconate in the Episcopal Church is tied, in part, to the actual functioning of persons as deacons whether openly acknowledged or not. There have been those laity in religious orders and in such organizations as the Church Army who have represented *diakonia* in lives of active charity. Undoubtedly, the definition of the diaconate is fuzzy at its boundaries. It is not easy to answer the question as to where the diaconate leaves off and the laity begins and this is as it must be for there is no absolute division between the orders of ministry in the church. As we have been suggesting, deacons are laity designated for special ministries of service. Lay people are also deacons in-so-far as they practice *diakonia*. This realization is vital to the mission of the church.

Having said this, it is requisite to acknowledge that while the kinds of leadership that deacons provide may vary according to the persons and needs involved, what they do as deacons is prescribed by law and custom. Too often in the past their activities have been too narrowly defined by priests who urgently needed relief in the performance of their tasks in relation to the ministry at the altar and the visitation of the sick and others prevented from attending church. While this may be quite legitimate and reflects a felt-need, it may be questioned whether the clergy understand the diaconate and recognize the unmet calls for *diakonia* in their own parishes. There has always been the danger of the priesthood distorting the diaconate, failing to recognize its essential character. Truly sensitive, aware priests will make more and better use of the time and talents of their laity in order to free the deacon for *diakonia*. In the best cases, and some of those are described below, the deacons are truly deacons, meeting actual needs in local congregations in ways that do justice to the gifts for *diakonia* which deacons possess —and do it with the support and encouragement of priests who stand ready to follow their leadership.

The deacons are not primarily priests' assistants. They are, ideally, bishops' assistants, men and women available to assist bishops in their diaconal ministry to the church and to the wider world, people committed to share in meeting diocesan needs, arousing and guiding the church at large in that servant ministry rooted in Christ's ministry. Consider what it could mean to bishops conscious of their diaconal responsibilities to have one or more deacons in each parish and mission ready and able— with due consideration to their various responsibilities—to respond to the bishop's call to service anywhere in the diocese. In one major American city a racial incident caused the religious leaders of the city to establish a covenant of racial and ethnic harmony, to labor for mutual understanding and cooperation, to promote peace and eliminate conditions promoting prejudice and violence. The covenant was promulgated in all of the churches and synagogues of the city and all people were enjoined to commit themselves to the covenant and to work to make it effective. The Episcopal bishop in that city would surely have benefited from being able to summon the deacons and direct them as "episcopal troops" to work on behalf of the covenant not only in the particular parishes where they normally served but anywhere in the diocese to which the bishop sent them. For this to be a realizable possibility it would be necessary for bishops, priests, laity and the deacons themselves, to recognize the deacons as "shock-troops" of the bishop in the service of *diakonia*. At the direction of the bishop, deacons could serve in crisis situations with effect. It must be noted here, however, that the initial responsibility rests with the bishops who are canonically responsible for their deacons and need to view their deacons as especially valuable resources, meet with them often and regularly both together and individually. This may be costly in terms of time for the individual bishop, but it possesses potential for providing bishops with more minds, hearts, hands and legs—more time instead of less—to develop and promote the church's essential character in service.

Why Ordination?

We have already considered some answers to this question, but it remains to say that ordination is a symbol linking the ordained ministries to the ministry of Jesus and signifying their dependence upon the activity of the Holy Spirit. Ordination witnesses to the true nature not only of the ordained ministries but of the church as a whole: the church is not created of itself, it is not simply a collection of like-minded people desirous of doing good. The church is the work of God. The community that we know as the church dispersed in innumerable communities is of God through Christ by the power of the Holy Spirit. The ordination of ministers witnesses to this fact—as does much else, including our baptism into Christ and thus into the priesthood of all believers.

This is to be balanced by the assertion that "the ordained ministry ought not in the first instance be an occupation or a profession; it is the product of a community." The report of a consultation on the theology of priesthood goes on to say: "In the heart of the ordained ministry is a pastoral leadership; it follows that a presbyter [with due consideration of the special relation between a bishop and a deacon we could include deacons here] is to be ordained when there is a community which calls or accepts that person as such." Christian tradition stands in opposition to the idea of an exclusively personal call to the ordained ministry.[8] The community, thus, plays a central role in ordination, recognizing the need for ordained ministry and choosing those who in the community's judgment seem best suited to meet the need.

To return to the other side of the argument, the person ordained at the direction of the community is not ordained solely to serve the particular place at which the ordination occurs. To be a deacon is to be ordained to the order of deacons, to serve the Lord, the church and the world, wherever the deacon is located now and in the future. This is important, for the community must recognize that the ministry of *diakonia* does not exist at the whim of a particular group of people who constitute its source. The ordained deacon is called to the ministry of service, which means that the deacon is then rooted, as a symbol must be, in that which is symbolized: the Servant Lord. Thus transcending the community—in this sense—the deacon is thrust into a position of leadership and is acknowledged, on account of the solemn rite of ordination, as a leader who serves, enabling the *diakonia* of the whole church. This involves saying and doing things which, at times, may meet with disapproval.

There is a further thought, which brings us back to the other side, the community side of our considerations. The consultation report indicates this by saying: "Hand in hand with the central role of the community goes the corollary that just as the entire community is a gathering of ministers serving one another in the world, so the ordained ministry is one of service. The ordained ministry is to serve the laity, not vice-versa."[9] The diaconate's distinctive role, that which is ordained by the church and empowered by the Spirit, is that of service to the church and through the church to the world.

To re-order our thoughts, the essential ministry is that of Christ. The church as a whole is the extension of that essential ministry in history. The church chooses or sets apart certain of its members for ordination as deacons, priests and bishops. Their ordained ministry is blessed and consists not in an hierarchically understood excercise of power *over* the church, but rather it consists of serving the church to more fully realize its essential character and mission in service. It is on this basis that the ordination of deacons is reasonable and—I would say on the basis of all of our considerations—compelling. Deacons symbolize the diaconal character of the church and by so doing, chosen by church (the entire *laos* of God) and ordained with the laying on of hands and prayer for empowerment by the Holy Spirit, minister to the benefit of all.

Deacons who engage in Diakonia

There are many deacons—and others—who exemplify *diakonia*. Here, as we conclude this study, we remember this fact. There can be no better way to do so than to cite actual persons, most of them ordained deacons in the Episcopal Church. And it is right to remember in relation to Matthew 25, a passage to which we have turned in earlier chapters.

> *"I was hungry and you gave me food,*
> *I was thirsty and you gave me drink . . .*
> *I was naked and you clothed me . . ."*

Jim Thompson is a deacon in the Diocese of Oregon. His daily employment finds him working as the Bishop's secretary, performing various functions, including overseeing postulants and candidates for Holy Orders and serving as registrar of the diocese. In addition, Deacon Thompson works on Sundays at St. Matthew's Parish in Portland, assisting with liturgical and preaching tasks. He is Chairman of Burnside Projects, a skid-row agency providing emergency shelter and clean-up facilities. Performing this ministry involves visiting in downtown hotels and bars (nights) and operating a soup-line Sunday nights with family and friends. Jim's family also operates an informal emergency shelter as part of their home. Leading a busy life, with much responsibility, Jim concludes, "I love it all!"

It is hardly necessary to point out that Jim's ministry has several directions, that it is concerned with feeding the hungry (soup-line, etc.) and providing the homeless with shelter. This ministry of *diakonia* on the streets is related to Jim's involvement in the liturgical life of his parish church and his secretarial work in the Bishop's office. Jim goes from the altar to serve the church and thence to serve the needs of the world; and he goes from the world of skid row to the church and to the altar bringing before the church and taking to God in prayer the needs of the world. There is a wholeness in his life and ministry which is the wholeness of those who serve the Servant Christ. We must also note that Jim's ministry enables *diakonia* in others, members of his family and those involved in Burnside Projects, as well as all of those who come in contact with the Bishop's office and those with whom he comes in contact in the parish church. Such is the ministry of *diakonia*.

"I was a stranger and you welcomed me . . ."

Eleanor Hill is a deacon and director of *Resonance*, a non-profit, ecumenical organization in Tulsa, Oklahoma, committed to a ministry to women by women. Established in 1977 in response to the need for a place and people ready and willing to help women in a constantly changing society, *Resonance* views itself as the church reaching out and ministering to women of all ages and with all sorts of problems, helping them to bring order and cultivate growth in their lives. Many who seek out *Resonance* have no church home and no active church affiliation. "We feel we become the church for them as they live through their pain and confusion." Housed in a building donated by St. John's Episcopal Church, "*Resonance* is a place where any women—either 'traditional' or 'liberated'—can feel comfortable. We try to be the supportive friend and a relaxed place where women can come for help. We belive we are the church acting out a statement of 'We're Aware and We Care.' "

Deacon Hill, as Director of *Resonance*, is responding to the expressed need of many women in our society. Great changes in the status of women have resulted in multitudes being alienated, becoming strangers in our midst. Many are suffering mental and physical abuse at the hands of angry men and are outcasts, cut off from family and friends, society, and all too often from the church as well. *Resonance*, like other such agencies, responds and is thus the means of genuine *diakonia*. Eleanor Hill is truly a deacon, serving women in need, enabling others in her position of leadership, and by her example inspiring others to identify their diaconal ministries.

Bill Arnold is chaplain to the Los Angeles Dodger Class A farm club at Vero Beach, Florida, the location of the Dodger Spring Training complex. Bill has been a deacon for about seven years, has assisted at Trinity Episcopal Church, helping with church services and visiting shut-ins. He is employed as a personnel services executive and in addition to assisting at his parish church has worked in his spare time with a correctional institution for young men, holding worship services and conducting sharing groups intended to help those incarcerated develop value aims and life goals. Most recently, as chaplain to the Vero Beach Dodgers, Bill has been ministering to baseball players and their families. This all began when, during a regular game, Bill saw a man slide into second base, colliding with a player from the visiting team. Both were injured, the visitor being taken away in an ambulance with a back injury. Bill says, "The Lord spoke to me, 'Who is ministering to these young men, particularly a young man like this who's away from home and might end up here in the hospital for some days after his team goes on? Who's tending to their spiritual needs?' I said, 'Lord, I don't know.' He said, 'Find out.' " Bill found out and was made team chaplain.

Bill's ministry embodies *diakonia*. He responded to evident need, welcoming the strangers, caring for them. Furthermore, he did this in such a way that he enabled others to develop their diaconal ministries, such as the Baseball Chapel coordinator for the team, a member of the team, other team members, the management and a young man who led a Bible Study group for the team and their families. He does this by exercising leadership gifts and skills and by providing a strong, winsome example. There he is in the locker room on Sunday evening before a game, leading the players in prayer, reading scripture and preaching God's saving Word, and they are all taking him most seriously, listening and praying.

"I was sick and you visited me."

John Burton is a business man, spending forty hours a week in conscientious fulfillment of his business responsibilities. Long associated with scouting, he is now a deacon-assistant at the Church of the Holy Trinity, Skokie, Illinois, where he serves "at God's altar every Sunday," preaches monthly, and visits the sick and shut-ins of the parish family. As an extension of his diaconal responsibilities in the parish, Deacon Burton has been engaged for the last five years in a hospital ministry at the North West Memorial Hospital, Chicago, one of the largest teaching hospitals in the Chicago area. As a Chaplain, working in his "spare time," John visits the sick, takes the sacrament to those who desire it, talks with patients and their relatives, and in general exhibits the concern and love of the Servant Christ.

John clearly and emphatically sees the dynamic relationship between his serving at the altar, his service in the parish, visiting the sick and shut-ins, and his hospital ministry. All is connected.

Dr. Francis D'Ambrosio is an ophthalmologist on the Active Staff of Emerson Hospital in Concord, Massachusetts. He is also a deacon in the Roman Catholic Church and as a member of St. Bernard's Church assists with Mass, preaches sermons, and officiates at weddings and baptisms. He emphasizes "that he cannot separate, 'being a deacon' from 'being a doctor' . . . 'I cannot preach a sermon on Sunday and forget about its message the rest of the week,' he said. 'I try to understand and interpret the Word of God to people as well as determine who and what I should be.'"[10] Deacon D'Ambrosio is exercising *diakonia* as a practicing ophthalmologist and has played a key role as chairman of the Medicine/Religion Committee of the hospital in establishing a chapel and furthering the work of chaplaincy.

In Dr. D'Ambrosio we have someone whose profession and ministry blend so obviously and completely that it is the wholeness that is perhaps most impressive in his example. And yet equally impressive is the public knowledge that this member of the hospital's medical staff, respected for his professional accomplishments, is an ordained deacon—something that cannot fail to have a beneficial impact on the hospital community, causing that community to take the chaplaincy of others more seriously and lending credibility to the religious issues involved in health care. At the hospital it is his diaconal status and work that stands out. At St. Bernard's the impressive thing is that this ordained minister, serving at the altar and preaching from the pulpit is a medical doctor who possesses healing skills. His witness in the parish is in part a testimony to the meaning of the faith to him, a meaning so vital that he does not hesitate to witness publicly.

"I was in prison and you came to me."

Jack Trembath was a Life and Health Insurance salesman in Michigan when he was ordained a deacon in 1976. From the outset he assisted the rector of his parish church in Mt. Clemens and that part of his ministry has continued to the present and is important to him. It was at the instigation of a Roman Catholic deacon that Jack became involved in the chaplaincy at the Macomb County Jail. After the Roman Catholic deacon left, and after an illness which permanently disabled him, bringing his sales career to an end, Jack began to spend more and more time at the jail. In time, with the support of the administration of the jail, Jack was made Chaplain and Volunteer Coordinator. He now cares from a daily prison population of 400 (which includes an overage of about 60), performing numerous tasks, conducting Sunday evening Eucharists, with the assistance of local priests and a resident choir, running Bible classes in both medium and maximum security sections of the jail, providing counseling services with the help of local clergy, seeing to it that those who are lonely in prison receive visitors, raising funds to assist needy prisoners, bringing the needs of prisoners to the attention of the administration, working to secure a full-time, fully funded chaplaincy program, and much else. Jack works with the correctional officers, counseling them as requested, preparing some of them to lead Bible classes, and in various ways enabling the diaconal ministries of those employed in the jail. His final task is to find a replacement whom he will assist to the degree that his declining health allows.

Once more we find a deacon performing a genuinely diaconal ministry and enabling others to realize their diaconal ministries whether they be ordained ministers or not. His title is significant: Jail Chaplain and Volunteer Coordinator. This might be translated as the Servant Christ's servant serving those in prison and enabling others to serve in such a way also. This ministry has blossomed in Jack's retirement years, which reminds us of the promise inherent in those whose secular employment has come to an end and who have much to live for and much to give, much strength yet, much experience, much caring, much *diakonia*.

JoAnn Marie Garma is a chaplain at the Orleans Parish Criminal Sheriff's Office in Louisiana. Specifically, she works full time at a prison, holding about 2,400 municipal and state prisoners, administered by Charles C. Foti, Jr., Criminal Sheriff. JoAnn is an active member of Grace Church, New Orleans, and has done most of what is required to be ordained a deacon. For JoAnn, however, the ordination process is not an end in itself.

Ordination will not identify her as a minister or her work as "ministry." She strongly believes that she is a minister whether ordained or not. Ordination will be meaningful for her as a recognition and blessing of the diaconal ministry which she is currently doing.

JoAnn's ministry is directed chiefly towards helping inmates, both male and female. Such services are often routine, such as assisting inmates when they leave to find jobs, places to live and, when needed, seeing that they have necessary clothing and a little money. JoAnn also facilitates clergy passes for clergy who desire to visit members of their congregations. More challenging is her work with volunteers who lead Bible study groups and worship. She supervises seminary students doing field work and soon will be involved with the Clinical Pastoral Education program at the prison, hoping to gain supervisory status. Most challenging is the counseling which she does as a part of her job. Some of this is done in group settings. In group counseling, JoAnn directly confronts dynamics which are intrinsic to prisons generally: suspicion and distrust. Although both are necessary and by-in-large healthy when dealing with persons who have broken the law, suspicion and distrust can impede personal growth and cause tensions to rise among the inmates. Within the confines of the group experience JoAnn encourages the inmate to examine his motivation which lies behind his need to be suspicious and to distrust. What are the games being played? What other alternative does he have? Where is his responsibility? As the inmate looks at himself and who he is, he invariably looks at his ability to trust or distrust, not only others but himself as well. Through this process JoAnn has observed some growth in the ability to trust, some motivation to take charge and be a responsible person. She has also observed that tensions, which her group members have experienced with other inmates in their living areas, are better managed. She hopes that the experiences within the group will develop in better relationships among the inmates. JoAnn also counsels individuals. She strongly believes in becoming involved in the counseling sessions. As stated, she does this through confrontation. At the same time she herself becomes transparent. She shares who she is, her humanness. This involves her strengths as well as her weaknesses, her foibles and past failures as well as her tenacity and achievements. As the inmate tells his story, she identifies with the story in some way with an experience from her own personal history. Through the process of involvement and sharing the inmate may come to believe that he too can change and grow. He too can "make it" in the world on his own. JoAnn has observed disturbing as well as gratifying insight on the part of the inmate which has challenged the inmate to grow. In the counseling process JoAnn finds that she grows as well. She believes that when effective counseling takes place both she and the inmate grow. "In terms of the Christian faith we both experience the Holy Spirit and are renewed. This is a most humbling, exciting experience." Chaplain Garma works with the staff as well as the prisoners, counseling when requested to do so, visiting staff when they are sick. One point of identification which JoAnn has with the staff is that she is "one of them." Under Sheriff Foti's direction she attended a training academy and is now herself a Deputy, serving as such for a brief period alongside other deputies; however, she sees herself and is viewed by inmates and others, first of all, as chaplain. In serving staff she serves people who work under considerable stress and, as a result, are prone to burn-out. JoAnn knows what that means for she too has her moments of almost intolerable stress and has suffered burn-out. Now, she knows when to stop, and often, when moments of great stress occur, she is ministered to and renewed. She is often this someone for others. She knows the meaning of mutual ministry.

JoAnn is a deacon although not ordained as such. She serves Christ by serving those in prison and those responsible for their retention and care. She serves by enabling others to serve, staff and volunteers. She serves through participation in ministry with others, admittedly being served not only by other staff but by prisoners too. What would her ordination as a deacon achieve? Amongst other things, as she believes, it would be a blessing and recognition of her diaconal ministry. It would also be a way in which the church would be witnessing more clearly and forcefully to the fact that diakonia is the very being of the church and law of human kind.

One further example is in order here, not as directly related to Matthew 25 as the others. Josephine Borgeson, a seminary trained deacon has worked since 1975 with the total ministry program of the Diocese of Nevada. In her position she has been responsible for a number of things, including campus ministry

and diocesan camp programming, as well as working on education in ministry. She now coordinates a training-in-ministry
program, shares supervision of several small congregations,
and is an active member of the Commission on Ministry for
Nevada. Phina, as she is called, is a teacher-enabler of ministry
and ministries. Educational tasks consume much of her time
and talents developing adult education materials and methods,
teaching in TEAM (teach each a ministry) Academy centers,
convening a preacher-in-training group and a parish pastoral
care team, and much, much more.

Josephine assesses her own ministry by asking "does this
act/project/program, etc., multiply ministries?" In her mind is
the statement that a servant leader is one who enables others
to become servant leaders. She believes that there is "real
symbolic strength in a deacon doing my job. While I may at times
have a high profile role as teacher or preacher, there is no
question of my being a presider, and hence less temptation to
be a leader who is presidential in style . . . Both my office and
my gender make it more difficult for people to lay traditional
clerical role expectations on me, so that it is easier for us to
develop mutual servant leadership among professionals in ministry (including clergy), locally called and trained clergy, and
laity." Phina provides a model for what deacons can be and do
as enablers of *diakonia*.

A Time for Adventure

The times in which we live call for adventure. The challenges
facing the church in our time necessitate not one venture but
many ventures in the renewal of the servant character of the
people of God. We have met some people who have ventured in
service. Most of them have been ordained deacons in the
Episcopal Church, but that is not the main point. In various
different ways Jim, Eleanor, Bill, John, Francis, Jack, JoAnn and
Phina have all exercised that *diakonia* which is at the heart of
Christian identity. In our experience we have met many more
such people, many similar to those discussed and many quite
different. There are those who have established and run hospices, ministering to the dying in personally affirming ways;
there are those who have concentrated their energies on ministering to minorities, such as Hispanic-Americans, and in

assisting refugees who live and work in our country; there are those who have ministered to divorced persons and their dependents, helping them to pass beyond anger and grief to new, creative lives; and so on and on. There are those whose professions are diaconal in nature, law enforcement officers, fire fighters, health care personnel, teachers, lawyers and professional ministers, whose activities take on a new and amazing power for good when identified with the ministry of the Servant Christ. There are administrators and financiers, business people of divers kinds, diplomats and politicans dedicated to making effectual that *diakonia* which we regard as every Christian's goal. There is no end to the examples around us. To be in Christ, through baptism, by faith with the working of God's Spirit in us, is to serve not only in formal worship but in our daily occupations and throughout all of life. Influenced by the example of the Servant Christ an amazing variety of people engaged in a wondrous variety of occupations are venturing in lives of sacrificial service. The hope of the world rests with them and with myriads following after them in ever growing and influential numbers and ways.

Nor should we expect that there should be any one movement or idea effectually operative in realizing the vision of the Servant Church. If they are truly of the essence of the church addressing the vital needs of the world, all movements will serve to cultivate *diakonia*. Movements as various as those dedicated to the ministry of the laity, mutual ministry, the mission of the church, liturgical renewal, spiritual formation, women's liberation, civil rights, and many more are not fully that which they can be and must be until they issue in *diakonia*, and such *diakonia* as flows from and returns to the God who made us, redeemed and redeems us, and gives us the life-giving Spirit.

The renewal of the diaconate in our day is one means towards the realizing of the vision, but it is a vital means, for, as we have seen, it is a peculiar—although not the exclusive—instrument for the enablement of diaconal ministry everywhere. The renewal of the diaconate calls for the renewal of the episcopate, the presbyterate/priesthood and the laity, for there can be no realization of the true nature of the diaconate without the renewal of the church in general.

Furthermore, insofar as the diaconate is concerned, there are various routes towards renewal. Some of those concerned for renewal will pursue it in relation to the parish-based diaconate. Others will seek for restoration of the ancient relation between bishops and their deacons. Still others will venture upon new routes as yet unimagined. We shall need not only tolerance of such variety, patience with one another, but encouragement, especially in the pursuit of new ventures in *diakonia*. It is the end or purpose that matters most and should direct our divers courses. The end is *diakonia*, the realization of the Servant ministry of Christ, which involves obedience to the very law of humankind: sacrificial service.

Questions for Study and Discussion

The following questions could be used by an individual or a study group. Study groups might wish to work on each chapter in a separate session. There would thus be five sessions, but I have added questions for a sixth. It would be vitally important for all members of the study group to have read the assigned chapter in advance and to have considered the questions posed for that chapter. It might be helpful to have particular persons assigned to start off discussion. It may be that there are too many questions for the time allotted, in which case the leader and/or the group should decide which of the possible questions will be discussed. In connection with the fifth session the group may want to have a deacon involved in the discussion. Indeed, it would be appropriate and helpful to have a deacon present as leader or participant in all sessions.

Session One: Chapter 1. The Church in the Present.
1. What is the present situation of the world? What are its dangers? What are its possibilities?
2. What is the present situation of the church? What are its dangers? What are its possibilities?
3. How is the Church challenged to respond to the world situation?

Session Two: Chapter 2. The Biblical Vision of the Church as Servant.
1. What do we learn from the New Testament concerning Christ's understanding of service (diakonia)?
2. What does the New Testament teaching on service have to say to us and our lives in Christ? As individuals? As church? As citizens?
3. How is worship (leitourgia) related to service (diakonia)?
4. What does 2 Corinthians 4:1-15 have to say about service and the ordained officers of the church, bishops, priests and deacons?

Session Three: Chapter 3. The Servant Church through History.
1. With reference to specific instances as recounted in this chapter, how has the church's identity as servant found expression in history? How has it been hindered? How fostered?

101

2. What was the sixteenth century English ideal of the servant church—especially as expressed in Prayer Book worship?

3. What was the relation between the evangelical revivals in eighteenth and nineteenth century America and service (*diakonia*)?

4. What is the relation between conversion and confession (*metanoia*) and service?

Session Four: Chapter 4. Thoughts Concerning the Vision Now.

1. Why should we prefer the "spherical" to the "hierarchical" understanding of the church and its ministry?

2. How are the ministries of bishops, priests and deacons diaconal—presenting the Servant Lord and enabling servant ministry?

3. What positive values are to be found in the servant image of the church?

4. What is the role of the servant ministry in the world?

Session Five: Chapter 5. Realizing the Vision.
                                 The Diaconate and the Church.

1. What arguments does this chapter present for the maintaining and renewal of the diaconate in the church?

2. In what ways can a revival of the diaconate be of practical value to the church?

3. What is ordination? Why should deacons be ordained?

4. How do the deacons and others presented as examples in this chapter carry on Christ's servant ministry?

5. Is this a time for adventure in the church? If so, what possible ways are suggested at the end of the chapter? What other possibilities are there?

Session Six: Application and Conclusion of Study.

1. What does this book suggest in terms of my life, the life of my parish church, the life of my community?

2. Do I regard my ministry as an extension of Christ's servant ministry? If so, in what ways do I serve God and neighbor? In what ways can I better serve God and neighbor?

3. Do I view the church and its ordained officers hierarchically —as exercising power above and apart from me? In what ways can this be defended? In what ways is such a view of danger to me and the church?

4. How does consideration of service (*diakonia*) alter thinking about the church and the ministry of all the people of God?

Notes

Chapter 1. The Church in the Present

[1]Philip Potter, "Science and Technology: Why Are the Churches Concerned," *Faith and Science in an Unjust World*, Report of the World Council of Churches' Conference on Faith, Science and the Future, July 1979, Vol. 1: Plenary Presentations, ed. by Roger L. Shinn (Geneva: Church and Society, World Council of Churches, n.d.), p. 22.

[2]Mihajlo Lesarovic and Eduard Pestel, *Mankind at the Turning Point: The Second Report to the Club of Rome* (New York: E. P. Dutton and Co., Inc./Reader's Digest Press, 1974), p. 147; see also p. 11.

[3]Ervin Laszlo et al., *Goals for Mankind: A Report to the Club of Rome on the New Horizons of Global Community* (New York: E. P. Dutton, 1977), p. 375.

[4]Ibid., p. 376.

[5]Jay W. Forrester, "Churches at the Transition Between Growth and World Equilibrium," *Zygon: Journal of Religion and Science*, Vol. 7, No., 3, p. 163.

[6]F. M. Esfandiary, "Homo Sapiens, the Manna Maker," *New York Times*, August 9, 1975, op. ed. page.

[7]Cited by Garrett Hardin, "The tragedy of the commons," *Notes for the Future: An alternative history of the past decade*, ed. by Robin Clarke (New York: Universe Books, 1976), p. 68.

Chapter 2. The Biblical Vision of the Church as Servant

[1]*Church Dogmatics*, IV, 2 (Edinburgh: T. & T. Clark, 1958), p. 692; see also IV (3), 2, pp. 889-890.

[2]*Gorgias*, 491e, B. Jowett trans., *The Dialogues of Plato*, I (New York: Random House, 1937). Much of the word study is based on Beyer's article in G. Kittel's *Theological Dictonary of the New Testament*, ed. G. W. Bromiley (Grand Rapids: Eerdmans, 1964-76). I have also consulted the pertinent words in G. Lampe's *Patristic Greek Lexicon* (Oxford: Clarendon Press, 1961).

[3]See Kittel, sub *diakoneō*, p. 83: "When Rabban Gamaliel II, the son of the rabbi, served other rabbis reclining at table with him, this caused astonishment. But Rabbi Jehoshua observed (Qid., 32b, cf. M. Ex., 18, 12): 'We find that a greater than he served at table. Abraham was greater than he, and he served at table.' A third added: God spreads the table before all men, and should not Rabban Gamaliel therefore . . . stand and serve us?"

[4]Of course, strictly speaking Mark 10:45 concerns that which is required of the Son of man in order that the Kingdom of God may be

brought in. But a universal application of the teaching is not erroneous, for the New Testament understanding of the Kingdom of God as God's rule and God's reign over all involves all that we mean by redemption, salvation and eternal life.

[5]See John E. Booty, "George Herbert, *The Temple*, and the *Book of Common Prayer*," *Mosaic* XII/2 (Winter 1979), pp. 75-90.

[6]See Richard Buckle, *Jacob Epstein Sculptor* (Cleveland and New York: World Publishing Co., 1963), pp. 99-100, 384-86.

[7]The idea of sacrifice is prominent in the theology of F. D. Maurice. See John E. Booty, *The Church in History* (New York: Seabury Press, 1979), pp. 138-140 and Maurice's *The Doctrine of Sacrifice* (1954).

[8]Concerning nature, the "socio-biologist" E. O. Wilson, has written suggestively of altruism in nature and human nature. See his *On Human Nature* (Cambridge: Harvard University Press, 1978), Ch. 7. Altruism, which Wilson defines as "generosity without hope of reciprocation" (p. 149), involves what we have been thinking of as sacrificial service.

[9]I have been influenced by John V. Taylor's understanding of "awareness" in *The Go-Between God* (Philadelphia: Fortress Press, 1973), esp. p. 19: "The Holy Spirit is that power which opens eyes that are closed, hearts that are unaware and minds that shrink from too much reality. If one is open towards God, one is open to the beauty of the world, the truth of ideas, and the pain of disappointment and deformity."

[10]Frederick Maurice, ed., *The Life of Frederick Denison Maurice*, II (New York: Charles Scribner's Sons, 1884), p. 394.

[11]*A Theological Word Book of the Bible*, ed. Alan Richardson (New York: Macmillan Co., 1951), p. 225.

[12]See William Nichols, *Jacob's Ladder: The Meaning of Worship*, Ecumenical Studies in Worship, 4 (Richmond, Va.: John Knox Press, 1958), p. 15.

[13]Franklin Young, "The Theological Context of New Testament Worship," *Worship in Scripture and Tradition*, ed. M. H. Shepherd (New York: Oxford University Press, 1963), p. 90.

[14]*Church Dogmatics* IV, 2, pp. 697-8.

[15]Anthony T. Hanson, *The Church of the Servant* (London: SCM Press, Ltd., 1962), p. 60. I am indebted to Hanson's book more than is indicated by this one reference here.

Chapter 3. The Servant Church Through History

[1]J. G. Davies, *The Making of the Church* (London: Skeffington and Son, Ltd., 1960), p. 17.

[2]*City of God*, X.6, as translated in Gerhart B. Ladner, *The Idea of Reform* (Cambridge: Harvard University Press, 1959), p. 280.

[3]Ibid., p. 281.

⁴*The Apostolic Tradition of Hippolytus*, trans. by B. S. Easton (Cambridge: At the University Press, 1934), p. 44.

⁵Ibid., p. 47.

⁶Ibid., p. 56.

⁷*Dialogue with Trypho*, 110, 3; in J. Stevenson, *A New Eusebius* (London: S.P.C.K., 1957), p. 61.

⁸*Apology*, I, 16; Ibid.

⁹*Contra Celsum*, III, 9; III, 30; *Comm. in Math.*, XVI, 8.

¹⁰*De Lapsis*, 5, 6; *New Eusebius*, pp. 229-30.

¹¹In *Creeds, Councils, and Controversies*, ed. J. Stevenson (New York: Seabury Press, 1966), pp. 4-6.

¹²Cited in C. N. Cochrane, *Christianity and Classical Culture* (London: Oxford University Press, 1944), p. 347.

¹³Translated by H. Bettenson, *Documents of the Christian Church* (London: Oxford University Press, 1943), pp. 152-3.

¹⁴*Conferences of Cassian*, I, 4-10; *Western Asceticism*, ed. Owen Chadwick, LCC 12 (Philadelphia: Westminister Press, 1958), pp. 196-201.

¹⁵Joseph A. Jungmann, S.J., *The Mass of the Roman Rite*, trans. by F. A. Brunner (New York: Bensiger Brothers, 1950), 1:91.

¹⁶Ibid., 1:129-132.

¹⁷Catherine of Sienna, *The Dialogue*, trans. S. Noffke, O.P. (New York: Paulist Press, 1980), p. 103.

¹⁸Ibid., p. 76.

¹⁹Ibid., p. 113.

²⁰Ibid., p. 121. Cf. Math. 25:40.

²¹Ibid.

²²In William Maskell, *Monumenta Ritualia Ecclesiae Anglicanae* (Oxford: At the Clarendon Press, 1882), 3:299.

²³*The First and Second Prayer Books of Edward VI* (London: J. M. Dent and Sons; New York: E. P. Dutton and Co., 1949), p. 399.

²⁴Ibid., p. 406.

²⁵Ibid., pp. 444, 453, 460.

²⁶Ibid., p. 454.

²⁷Ibid., pp. 461-2.

²⁸Ibid., p. 463.

²⁹Ibid., p. 382.

³⁰On this and what follows see *The Godly Kingdom of Tudor England*, ed. J. Booty (Wilton, Conn.: Morehouse-Barlow, 1981), esp. chaps. 1 and 2.

³¹Ibid., p. 37. This is an application of Luke 22.

³²*Lawes*, V. 56.10; cited in *The Spirit of Anglicanism*, ed. W. J. Wolf (Wilton, Conn.: Morehouse-Barlow, 1979), p. 35.

³³*Lawes*, V. 56.11; ibid.

[34]See J. Booty, "The Bishop Confronts the Queen: John Jewel and the Failure of the English Reformation," in *Continuity and Discontinuity in Church History*, ed. F. F. Church and T. George (Leiden: E. J. Brill, 1979), pp. 215-31.

[35]Jewel, *Works*, PS (Cambridge: At the University Press, 1845-50), 2:1123-24.

[36]Maurice, *The Doctrine of Sacrifice* (London, 1893), pp. 220-1. I have drawn on my chapter, "Christian Spirituality: From Wilberforce to Temple," in the forthcoming *Anglican Spirituality*, ed. W. J. Wolf (Wilton, Conn.: Morehouse-Barlow, 1982) for my discussion here of Maurice, Temple and Underhill.

[37]Temple, *Fellowship with God* (London: Macmillan, 1930), p. 218.

[38]Temple, *Christianity and the Social Order* (London: S.C.M. Press, 3rd ed., 1950), pp. 57-58.

[39]Underhill, *The Life of the Spirit and the Life of To-day* (New York: E. P. Dutton, 1922), p. 271.

[40]Cited in E. Clowes Chorley, *Men and Movements of the Episcopal Church* (New York: Charles Scribner's Sons, 1946), p. 7.

[41]R. S. Emrich, *Earth Might be Fair* (New York: Harper and Brothers, 1945), p. 103.

[42]W. S. Sweet, *Religion in the Development of American Culture, 1765-1840* (New York: Charles Scribner's Sons, 1952), pp. 235-236.

[43]In *The Catholic Revival and the Kingdom of God* (Milwaukee: Morehouse, 1934), pp. 70-71.

[43]See Donald B. Meyer, *The Protestant Search for Political Realism, 1919-1941* (Berkeley and Los Angeles: University of California Press, 1960).

[45]A. T. Mollegen, *Christianity and Modern Man. The Crisis of Secularism* (Indianapolis: Bobbs-Merrill, Co., 1961), pp. 152-3.

Chapter 4. Thoughts Concerning the Vision Now

[1]Innocent III, *Selected Letters Concerning England*, C. R. Cheney and W. H. Semple, eds. (London: Nelson, 1953), p. x.

[2]Congar, *Ministeres et communion ecclesiale* (Paris: du Cerf, 1971), p. 37, as found in an unpublished paper by Joseph A. Komochak called "The Permanent Diaconate and the Variety of Ministries in the Church," p. 17.

[3]Hooker, *Works* (Oxford, 1888), 3:695-696.

[4]From an unpublished paper by Wesley Frensdorff, Bishop of the Episcopal Church in Nevada, p. 1.

[5]Jones, "New Vision for the Episcopate?" in *Theology*, 81 (July, 1978), p. 285.

[6]Ibid., p. 286.

[7]Frensdorff, unpublished paper, p. 2.

[8]*Book of Common Prayer* (1979), p. 336.

[9]Ibid., p. 534.

[10]See Hooker, *Lawes*, V.lxxviii. 3 (*Works*, 1888, 2:472).

[11]Frensdorff, "Holy Orders and Ministry: Some Reflections," in *The Anglican Theological Review*, 59 (July, 1977), p. 288.

[12]*Book of Common Prayer* (1979), p. 545.

[13]This is from an unpublished "Report to the Bishop of Massachusetts Re: Permanent," June 1980, p. 2.

[14]*Book of Common Prayer* (1979), p. 328.

[15]Hooker, *Lawes*, II.1.4 (*Works*, 1888, 1:290).

[16]*Explanatio Apocalypsis*, II, cited in Henri de Lubac, *The Splendour of the Church* (New York: Sheed and Ward, 1956), p. 74.

[17]In that which immediately follows I wish to acknowledge the inspiration of an unpublished paper by Avery Dulles, S.J., entitled "Imaging the Church for the 1980's," delivered in New York in June, 1980. Professor Dulles prefers to image the church as the Community of Disciples but what he has to say agrees well with the image of the church as Servant.

[18]See Arnold Toynbee, *Mankind and Mother Earth, a Narrative History of the World* (New York and London: Oxford University Press, 1976), p. 5. The term was coined by Teilhard de Chardin.

[19]*Man and Nature*, Hugh Montifiore, ed. (London: Collins, 1975), p. 4.

[20]Ibid., p. 77.

[21]Ibid., pp. 77-78.

[22]Ibid., pp. 78-79.

[23]See, for instance, Ann Crittenden, "A World to Feed," a series which began in the *New York Times*, Sunday, August 16, 1981, p. 1, and Robert Reinhold, "Water in America: Solving the Quandary," which began in the *New York Times*, Sunday, August 9, 1981, p. 1.

[24]See James J. Young, CSP, "Divorce Ministry," in *Models of Ministry* (National Assembly of Women Religious, 1979), pp. 24-31.

[25]Barth, *Church Dogmatics*, IV/3, eds. G. W. Bromiley and T. F. Torrance (Edinburgh: T. & T. Clark, 1961), pp. 663-664.

[26]See James B. Ashbrook, "No Longer One by One: Ministry to Structures," in *Explorations in Ministry*, G. Doyglass Lewis ed. (New York: IDOC, 1971), pp. 14-26.

[27]See, for instance, Jay W. Forrester, "Churches at the Transition Between Growth and World Equilibrium," *Zygon*, 7, 3, pp. 165-166 where he discusses "potential evil in humanitarianism."

Chapter 5. Realizing the Vision
The Diaconate and the Church

[1]*Book of Common Prayer*, 1979, p. 510.

[2]*Oxford American Prayer Book Commentary* (New York: Oxford University Press, 1950), pp. 527-529.

[3]See the Apostolic Letter of Pope Paul VI, *Sacrum Diaconatus Ordinem* (June 18, 1967) and the 3rd session of the 90th General Congregation (September 29, 1964).

[4]Study Text, National Conference of Catholic Bishops, p. 13. On the history of the diaconate through the fourth century see James M. Barrett, *The Diaconate: A Full and Equal Order* (New York: Seabury, 1981).

[5]Paul Tillich, *Systematic Theology*, I (Chicago: University of Chicago Press, 1951), pp. 239, 240.

[6]Komonochak, "The Permanent Diaconate," unpublished paper, B15.

[7]Vatican II, *Ad gentes*, 16.

[8]Toward a Theology of Priesthood, unpublished paper of Trinity Institute (New York, [1981]), p. 6.

[9]Ibid.

[10]"More than a Clinician," *Emerson Quarterly*, Autumn '81, p. 13.